Memories
of a
NONYA

D1446933

Memories
of a
NONYA

Queeny Chang

 Marshall Cavendish
Editions

Cover design by Adithi Khandadai Shankar
On the cover: Miniature portrait of the author painted in 1917 by Eva Ward.

© 2016 Marshall Cavendish International (Asia) Private Limited
Text © Queeny Chang

This book was first published in 1981. This edition is based on the 1982 edition
published by Eastern Universites Press.

This edition published by Marshall Cavendish Editions
An imprint of Marshall Cavendish International
1 New Industrial Road, Singapore 536196

Other Marshall Cavendish Offices:
Marshall Cavendish Corporation. 99 White Plains Road, Tarrytown NY 10591-
9001, USA • Marshall Cavendish International (Thailand) Co Ltd. 253 Asoke,
12th Flr, Sukhumvit 21 Road, Klongtoey Nua, Wattana, Bangkok 10110, Thailand
• Marshall Cavendish (Malaysia) Sdn Bhd, Times Subang, Lot 46, Subang Hi-Tech
Industrial Park, Batu Tiga, 40000 Shah Alam, Selangor Darul Ehsan, Malaysia

Marshall Cavendish is a trademark of Times Publishing Limited

National Library Board, Singapore Cataloguing-in-Publication Data

Name(s): Chang, Queeny, 1896- | Marshall Cavendish Editions, publisher.
Title: Memories of a Nonya / Queeny Chang.
Description: Singapore : Marshall Cavendish Editions, [2016] |
"This book was first published in 1981. This edition is based on the
1982 edition published by Eastern Universities Press."
Identifier(s): OCN 944464978 | ISBN 978-981-47-5157-5 (paperback)
Subject(s): LCSH: Chang, Queeny, 1896- | Malaysia--Biography. |
China--Biography.
Classification: LCC CT1568.C48 | DDC 959.505092--dc23

Printed in Singapore by Markono Print Media Pte Ltd

To the memory of my father

Contents

'Though nothing can bring back the hour
Of splendour in the grass
And glory in the flower
We will grieve not:
rather find strength in what remains behind.'

—Wordsworth

⚜ *Publisher's Note*

QUEENY CHANG (1896–1986) was the daughter of Tjong A Fie, a prominent businessman and leader of the Chinese community in Medan, Indonesia. She was born into a life of luxury and married into a prominent Chinese family from Amoy, China. From a young age, she was exposed to different cultures and people, and she was fluent in German, Dutch, French, Malay, Chinese as well as several dialects.

A pioneer in many ways, Queeny's biography gives readers a realisic idea of what life was like in the early 20th century. She also shares interesting portraits of the relationship with her immediate family as well as friends.

The late Queeny Chang with the 1982 edition of her book.

Queeny Chang wrote her biography in Medan. Entitled *Memories of a Nonya,* it was first published by *The Star* in 1981. It was re-published by Eastern Universities Press in 1982.

After *Memories of a Nonya* was published, Queeny spent most of her time in Medan. She suffered a mild stroke in 1983 and relocated to Singapore where her grandson, Lam Seng (Tong's son), and her grand daughter-in-law, Poo Ten, took care of her until her death on 28 August 1986.

In early 2016, Poo Ten approached Marshall Cavendish to consider a re-issue of *Memories of a Nonya.* In this edition of the book, we have retained the spelling of words as per the original edition. As an example, nonya is used instead of nyonya which is the spelling of the word today.

Queeny Chang at home in Medan.

Foreword

NONYAS ARE A vanishing breed. A gracious but increasingly rare species of the old-world charm about whom too little is known.

So, when one of them dares to commit her memories to paper, it is something to look forward to. A publishing event, no less.

Queeny Chang's memories are all the more remarkable because she is a remarkable woman, and also because she has a fascinating story to tell. She tells it warmly, enthusiastically and authentically.

Queeny is a nonya who went to a Dutch school and became 'foreignised'. However, she never forgot her nonya origin. She spoke Malay as well as her Chinese dialect, Khek; and during her school vacations in Penang, picked up a smattering of nonya Hokkien.

I first met Queeny shortly after I had joined *The Star*, under its new management, towards the end of 1977. *The Star* had published the first part of her memoir earlier that year and she brought the second part to show me. We duly published them in February 1980 and the tremendous interest they created among the readers in Malaysia and the neighbouring countries prompted her to have her writings reproduced in a more permanent form. This book is the happy outcome.

Khor Cheang Kee
Editorial Adviser
The Star, Malaysia

Preface

AT THE RISK of being refused entry on account of my passport's expiration in twelve days, I had travelled from Jakarta to be in Penang in time for my brother Kian-liong's birthday in December 1976. Our niece and her family had motored up from Singapore besides several relatives who had arrived from Medan. In spite of all the fuss we had made expecting a celebration, Kian-liong wanted instead to make a pilgrimage to *Kek Lok Si*, a Buddhist temple in Ayer Itam, Penang, to take offerings to our father whose memorial image (statue) is kept, together with those of other prominent people, in a gilded shrine encased in glass in the Tower for Sacred Books. They were the first donors to the construction of the Temple at the end of the nineteenth century. Although the hall is not open to the public, we were admitted after we had explained our wish to the guardian monk.

I saw the life-like statues displayed in colourful Mandarin outfits when I first visited the place in 1908 and often again in later years. Among these sculptures, besides my father, those known and related to us are great-uncle Tio Tiauw-set, Uncle Cheah Choon-seng and my uncle Tjong Yong-hian. We were happy to know that the names of our elders are still remembered with deference and their deeds praised warmly.

My uncle's name appears again on pillars of the Precious Hall of Buddha and on the blackened rocks alongside the beautiful archway.

This pilgrimage evoked the idea of writing this book — a dedication to the memories of my beloved father who gave me the best years of my life.

Queeny Chang

Part One

1

Kwan Yin, Goddess of Mercy and Complaisance, saves the Ugly Duckling

IN THE peaceful surroundings of *Chanteclair*, a picturesque bungalow on a slope of the mountain resort Brastagi, I sat facing the brown peaks of the proud Volcano Sibayak, its white smoke merging into the blue morning sky. Wrapped in the sweet perfume of roses and jasmines, one's mind is cleansed of all the impurities of worldly desires and can only lose itself in serene and endearing thoughts.

Suddenly, as if awoken from a dream long gone-by, the carefree days of my childhood beckoned me. In this kaleidoscope of tender recollections, the first image to emerge from a varied and glorious past is that of my mother, young and beautiful, impregnated with devotion for her family and home.

It was the year 1902. I was about six years old, a not too pretty girl with a pale square face, a pair of melancholic eyes with scarce lashes that looked dreamy under thin straggly brows. I had a flat nose and two of my front teeth were missing. And on top of all those imperfections, a head showing patches of baldness. Poor me, I had just recovered from typhoid. However unattractive I might have appeared in other people's eyes, in my mother's I was a perfect creation, which had almost slipped through her hands, were it not for her devoted care.

For forty days and nights she had sat by my bed, feeling the burning of my fever, wiping away my cold sweat, changing my clammy clothes, giving me medicine every three hours as ordered by the doctor. Neglecting food and sleep, she had sat with gloomy eyes, more often filled with tears than dry, watching the raving little creature swinging between life and death. Though near to exhaustion, my mother had refused to entrust me, a vacillating candle which at any moment might extinguish, into other hands. Especially so when on one occasion, a male nurse engaged to relieve her had by mistake, given me turpentine instead of my medicine. I can clearly remember the doctor's furious face when he smelled its odour in my mouth while making his evening call. Asked what he had given me, the nurse produced the bottle. Pointing his finger at the frightened nurse, the doctor shouted in a thunderous voice: 'Out, you!' I watched the commotion around me: the doctor grumbling, my mother crying, my father pacing helplessly around the room in speechless anxiety. I was given a huge glass of milk and was none the worse for the experience, to the great relief of everybody. But since that occasion, my mother was not to be drawn away from the sick-room. Morning and night, she prayed to Kwan Yin, Goddess of Mercy and Complaisance. If no human power could save her child, the Goddess of Mercy could. Miraculously, her prayers were answered and I recovered. Since then, my mother became a devotee of the Goddess Kwan Yin. And there I was — the ugly duckling.

With permission from the doctor, my mother took me out for the first time since my illness on Chinese New Year's day. She had dressed me up like a doll, in a red silk jacket and trousers and red silk shoes. She hung a gold chain around my neck and put gold bangles on my wrists and ankles.

Together with my father and my little brother Fa-liong, we went to my uncle's house which was next to ours. Uncle Yong-hian and Aunt Liu were in the big hall waiting for visitors. After the formal kow-tows and offering of good wishes, my uncle drew me to his knees and said how pretty I looked. I smiled happily showing my missing teeth. My little brother merely received a slight pat on his head and no praise, so contrary to the privileged attention due to a male child. On this particular occasion, following my illness, I seemed to have become the centre of everyone's concern.

'Elder Brother,' said my father to my uncle, 'if this unworthy girl had not got well, I would have cancelled our New Year reception this evening, but as she is now better, I hope you and Sister-in-law will honour us with your presence.'

'Of course, of course,' answered my uncle effusively, 'we must celebrate Foek's happy recovery together.' My uncle liked to call my name as often as possible, because 'Foek' means luck. So much for the ugly duckling.

That evening, my mother dressed me in a batik sarong and *kebaya* like a native girl. She made a knot of the thin strands of discoloured hair on top of my head and inserted tiny diamond hairpins in it to keep it from falling apart. On my chest rested a diamond pendant and there were lovely little diamond bracelets and rings to match. My feet were shod in embroidered sandals. Thus attired, I could have been a little princess in the Sultan's household.

My mother herself was gorgeously dressed in her gala costume; *songket kebaya* and *kain*, made of wine-red handwoven silk interwoven with gold threads, a material specially made for the royal families. Overseas Chinese ladies had followed that fashion. Her glistening black hair was done in a round bun on top of her head and arranged with a row of diamond hairpins and small diamond flowers. Her *kebaya* was fastened with *kerungsang* — a set of three brooches of which the first and largest was in the form of a peacock with an open tail, followed by two smaller round ones pinned beneath it. That was the vogue followed by fashionable ladies in Penang and Medan.

My mother was much admired, standing there beside her husband who, himself, was an imposing figure. She was a complete mistress of the Malay language in which she conversed with foreigners.

She was perfectly at ease in the circle of invited dignitaries and people of diverse nationalities. It seemed as if she had

Author's mother dressed as Penang nonya.

never known otherwise. She was conscious of my father's position, and was determined to be worthy of him.

My father took me by the hand as he thanked the guests for their good wishes. Everyone had a kind word for me. The Resident took me up and held me so high that everybody could see me and kissed me on both cheeks. The Sultana embraced me and hugged me to her ample breasts. They all knew how much my parents loved me and were pleased to share in their happiness on my recovery. My father did not hide the fact that were I not better, there would have been no reception, the function everyone had looked forward to. It was a splendid and lavish affair and its success was awarded to the smiling duckling.

2

Country maiden becomes
lady of good fortune

ALTHOUGH THEY HAD had no formal education, both my father and uncle were greatly respected by the Dutch authorities for their valuable services as Captains of the Chinese population.

The Chinese in Indonesia, because of their willingness to work, their initiative and business acumen, had established themselves firmly into the economy. They, however, remained a separate and distinct community. They held to their own social traditions and customs, and their right to do so was acknowledged by the Dutch in the appointment of a Chinese Captain with independent jurisdiction in such matters. There were also Chinese lieutenants who were directly responsible to the Captain.

The Chinese were not like the Dutch, my mother told me often enough. Most Chinese, she said, were illiterate pioneers who brought very little money with them from their homeland to the new country seeking work on tobacco plantations. They were very badly treated and even the Chinese themselves called them 'sold pigs'. These contract labourers usually borrowed money from the rich on security; not of property, but on the person of the borrower. In effect, it was a form of debt slavery.

My mother had lived on a tobacco plantation before she married my father. Born in 1880, in the small town of Bindjei, Sumatra, my mother was uneducated. Her father was chief overseer in Sungei Memtjirim, one of the Deli Company's plantations where he supervised several hundred coolies. The Deli Company was, at the time, a large concern which had monopoly of the cultivation of tobacco in Sumatra. Therefore, she had spent her childhood on the estate as a country maiden knowing nothing of the city. Besides, she was brought up by a severe mother who stuck to the old fashioned ideas that a girl need not know more than cooking and baking cakes, her place being in the kitchen.

However, my mother was endowed with a rebellious nature and a grand spirit. To the extreme dislike of her mother, she often judged herself superior to her brothers — whether they were elder or younger, she did not care. She resented the idea that boys were preferred to girls. She quarrelled incessantly with the boys and her final words were always, 'You just wait and see, one day I'll shine over all of you.' And the retort would be: 'You think you're the wife of lieutenant Tjong A Fie (then a leading figure)?' Little did they know that one day those words, spoken at random, would come true!

Thus, my mother reached marriageable age without an offer for marriage. But one propitious morning, as if Fate had thrown in its lot, a matchmaker came from Medan to approach my grandfather, Lim Sam-hap, for my mother's hand to Tjong A Fie. Although my grandfather considered the proposal a great honour, he was hesitant because of the difference between their ages; my father was then a widower of 35 and my mother a mere girl of 16. My grandmother, on the contrary, was in favour of marrying off her unruly daughter as quickly as possible. She doubted that such a chance would ever occur again because my mother already had the reputation of being haughty and aggressive, due to her brothers' propaganda.

Young as she was, my mother was well aware that she was to become the wife of an authority; but instead of being subdued, she demanded to see the widower in person, so that she could talk to him herself. My grandmother was shocked; and thought her most unfeminine for wanting to meet the man before she was married to him but all her protests were waived and my father, though finding the demand most unusual, good-naturedly called at my grandmother's home.

A young girl with a proud countenance and vivid, intelligent eyes faced the prospective bridegroom unabashedly and regarded him from head to foot. She studied his personality, his mannerisms and speech. My father sat down on a chair facing his bride-to-be and in his deep voice told her that he had just lost his wife leaving three children: a boy of 15 and two girls of 12 and 11 respectively. He added frankly that he also had a wife in his village, Sung-kow, China; a girl his parents had chosen and whom he could not discard. As the village wife could not join him in Sumatra, having to look after his aged mother in China, he wished to marry her to replace the mother of his children.

My mother seemed satisfied with my father's honest explanation and moreover, my father's open and frank face had made a good impression on her. My father was good-looking and though in his mid-thirties, was still in the prime of his life. He was tall and well-built; with a square face, high intelligent forehead, and a high-bridged nose above a determined mouth. His complexion was of a glowing bronze. My mother consented to marry him on one condition: that after she became my father's wife, there would be no other secondary wife. My father gladly accepted her condition, because he saw in the young girl a strong and inspiring character, one who would not disgrace him but who would assist him in his ambition for higher achievements. So, my mother married my father according to ancient customs, wearing the traditional bridal costume and going through the ritual ceremony before the altar of God and the ancestors.

Contrary to her brothers' prediction that she would now be singing a tone lower, having an old husband to keep her head down, she would show them that all their mockery would turn in her favour.

When my father was promoted a few months after their marriage, my mother was considered an auspicious wife who brought luck and prosperity to her husband; and at my birth

12 months later, even though I was a girl, it was said that as the first-born was female, many male descendants would follow. Thus the former country maiden had turned out to be a Lady of Good Fortune.

Leaving me in the care of an old *amah*, my father took my mother to China to visit my grandmother in the village. My mother used to tell me how she was spoiled by my grandmother who called her 'my overseas daughter-in-law', making it clear that my mother's place was with my father and that of mother Lee, my father's village wife, was in the village to look after the house and the ricefields. Being autocratic, my grandmother knew how to keep the peace between her two daughters-in-law. She gave each of them to understand that their duties were equally important. Being a village girl, mother Lee was quite happy with the arrangement, because she could take pride in her importance of being entrusted with the riches of her husband.

As my grandmother's word was law, nobody dared to disobey her. Thus, after a sojourn of three months, my father and mother returned to Medan with many happy memories of my village grandmother.

3

The youth with the ruddy complexion

MY THOUGHTS ARE running helter-skelter and unconsciously the story of my father's early days, which my mother had learned from my village grandmother, slips back to mind.

Our forefathers were originally from central China. Owing to droughts, floods and incessant wars, they had drifted from one place to another until they reached the coast. When they finally settled in the provinces of Kwangtung and Fukien on the east coast, they were treated as visitors by the local inhabitants.

Among the exodus of farmers, tradespeople, artisans and warriors was also a group of scholars whose ancestry could be traced back to aristocrats; they had never known menial work. If by chance, a scholar could pass the Imperial Examination, he would become the pride and support of his clan. Sometimes, to save an entire family from perishing from hunger and illness, parents would sell their children to people who could give their offspring food and shelter.

My father's family was descended from one of these. His parents lived with all their cousins in a big house built when the family had been successful, generations back. Each family occupied one or two rooms and each had their own kitchen. The only place they shared was the Ancestral Hall where occasions like the New Year and births of male descendants were celebrated (the latter on the Lantern Festival, the fifteenth day of the first moon). My father grew up in these surroundings where pettiness and jealousy often resulted in quarrels and fights among the nearest of kin. He resented these conflicts immensely. However, since his early teens, he was frequently called upon to judge the differences which arose from these family disputes. My father never failed in his judgment because of his righteous character and exceptional intelligence. They all bowed to his decision.

My grandfather had a modest sundry shop where he sold daily provisions but the meagre earnings were hardly sufficient to feed a family of seven sons and one daughter. Therefore, my father's elder brother, Yong-hian, had already joined the pioneers and sailed to the Southern Seas.

After my grandfather's death, my father took over the sundry shop. But this did not appeal to him sufficiently to keep him in Sung-kow which had nothing to offer a genius who was destined for fame and greatness. He begged my grandmother again and again to let him join his brother in the Southern Seas. She finally consented, though with reluctance, because my father was her favourite son. He promised his mother that he would make good and return with gold and riches so that she could enjoy the twilight of her life in comfort and peace. With those words, he left her in the care of his youngest brother, determined to fulfill his promise.

Early one morning, a spirited youth of 18 with only ten silver dollars sewn in to his cotton waistband took the *sampan* down the river to Swatow and then embarked a big wooden junk sailing between the Southern Seas and the homeland (China).

All passengers, young and old, had different destinations and different trades. But they had one common aim — to seek a fortune. Some old-timers who had already settled down in various parts of the new world, like Borneo, Java, Malaya, Singapore and Sumatra, had many stories to tell about the hardships they had to endure before attaining what they now held — money earned with blood and sweat. Money which they brought back to the old village to buy padi fields and build a permanent home for their old age. My father listened to their stories with eagerness. He knew that even in the land of golden dreams, one could not succeed without hard work. Money did not grow on trees ready for

Paternal grandfather.

Paternal grandmother.

the picking; the tree itself had to be cultivated first before it could bear fruit.

Thus in the year 1880, after months of perilous sailing, my father landed in Labuhan, then an important town on the east coast of Sumatra, a sea link with the outside world. He found that my uncle had done well, being Chief of the Chinese community in the service of the Dutch government and bearing the title of lieutenant. It was not difficult for my uncle to introduce his brother, newly arrived from China, to his compatriots who were willing to oblige their Chief.

From the moment of their meeting, Tjong Sui-fo, a sundry shop owner, took to the young man who had an open countenance on which honesty and bravery were written. What struck him most was the young man's bronze complexion with a red glow which, according to astrology, he said, spelled position, power and wealth; something not to be overlooked. My father laughed at the analysis of his future and felt his waistband which contained his whole fortune; altogether ten silver dollars, each engraved with a dragon of the Manchu national mint.

My father was employed as a jack-of-all-trades. As he knew Chinese, he kept the books, served at the counter and ran errands in between. At the end of the month, he collected the bills to the great satisfaction of his employer, because there was never a cent unaccounted for. Most of all, he was praised for his ability to persuade difficult creditors to pay their arrears in his pleasant manner. My father befriended people of all nationalities in the mixed community: Malays, most of whom were *Tengkus* belonging to the royal family, Arabs, Indians and finally the Dutch whom he judged important for his ultimate aim — to be successful in the country they ruled. He learned to speak Malay which was the language spoken by every nationality.

Tjong Sui-fo was also a supplier to the local prison and whenever my father went there to deliver goods, he stopped to chat with the prisoners. He listened to their stories of injustice, of being imprisoned for no other crime than that of being members of the triad society, something which they considered very noble, loyal and brave. My father knew that it was unlawful to belong to a secret society and though he sympathised with their feelings, he deeply deplored his countrymen's ignorance. Some day, he thought, he hoped to be able to help them.

Gradually, my father gained trust and esteem in the small town and when the Chinese elders recommended him to be District Chief for the Chinese, the Dutch government fully approved. He left his job at the sundry shop and was well-rewarded by his employer. My father never forgot his former benefactor and even when, in later years, he had climbed to the pinnacle of success as Tjong Sui-fa had predicted, he treated the old man with deference and respect.

My father engaged himself wholeheartedly in his new career. He followed the government to Medan which was to become the new capital of the East Coast and was assigned an office of his own in a wooden building with an attap roof. Soon after, he was promoted to lieutenant while my uncle Yong-hian became Captain. Through the introduction of friends, my father married a Penang girl, the daughter of a well-known family of the Chew clan who was also one of the pioneers. She bore him three children, but unfortunately she died at the early age of 32.

※

4

Tjong A Fie's magnificent mansion

WHEN MY FATHER married my mother, he was staying temporarily at my uncle's house. His wooden house was being demolished and in its place a magnificent mansion was to rise. After three quarters of a century, it still stands, though it has lost much of its glory.

Not long after my parents returned from China, my mother gave birth to a son, but to her great grief the boy died in infancy. I have a vague vision of the baby lying on a table in the storeroom in my uncle's backyard. My mother was sitting in a corner crying.

The next day, the room was empty. I asked for my baby brother and was told by my old *amah* that he had gone — gone far away and would never come back. I was about three years old, but the memory of it has never faded. The following year, my mother bore her second son...

Our new house was completed and a propitious date was chosen for the move. Though I was barely five at that time, I have a vivid recollection of a procession at night, of men carrying innumerable Chinese lanterns to light the short distance from my uncle's house to ours. My uncle and my father were in the lead, followed by friends and relatives. Then came my aunt richly attired in *sarong kebaya* adorned with glittering diamonds. On one side of her walked my mother carrying my little brother Fa-liong in her arms, and on the other was a tall lady with a fair complexion wearing Chinese clothes, a rather loose black silk jacket and trousers. Her hair was done up on top of her head in something like a cone with a long gold pin stuck in the middle. She was holding me by the hand and I wondered who she was. I did not remember having seen her in my uncle's house and, judging from her appearance, thought she must be some relative newly arrived from China.

I did not see much of the ceremony performed at the front gate which was opened only when we arrived. A garden separated the house from the road. The house was brilliantly lit, from the wide porch to the interior of the beautiful building. It was a strange scene because I had never known the magic of electricity before this. Hitherto, I knew only the difference between an oil lamp and a candle. My eyes were blinded by the brilliance of the huge chandeliers which hung from the high painted ceiling of the big hall, spreading their radiance over the walls which held candelabra designed in the shape of flower buds. There was black wood furniture encrusted with mother-of-pearl. I had already seen one or two pieces of these in my uncle's home, but here were so many more and very beautifully polished. What my eyes saw at that time is difficult to describe. Everything was magnificent beyond words.

The ancestral hall was even more impressive. Everything was red and gold. Tables and chairs were covered with red satin covers embroidered with gold dragons and multi-coloured phoenix. The ancestors' shrine was in an elevated alcove. It was made of deep red wood with gold framework all around. In the centre stood three black and gold tablets inscribed with the names and ranks of the ancestors. Huge betasseled Chinese lanterns hung from the four corners of the hall and the walls were painted with pink peonies and plum blossoms.

An old white-haired man lighted two enormous red candles on the altar, then passed three long joss sticks to my uncle, who, as eldest in the family, was to perform the house warming ceremony. He knelt with reverence before the ancestors' shrine. I did not understand much of the rites which were conducted with great solemnity. The sombre atmosphere had made me nervous. Suddenly, due to the smoke of joss sticks and sandalwood (or perhaps my nervousness), I had a fit of sneezing and coughing. In the grave Ancestral Hall of the Big House stillness, the noise I made was horrible. I was terrified. My mother glared at me and her eyes seemed to order me to keep quiet, but the more I tried, the more I choked. Fortunately, the tall lady found a cup of tea someone had left on a side table, and gave it to me to drink. My choking subsided, but tears were running down my contorted face. At this crucial moment, the ceremony came to an end, and I was happily relieved.

People began to crowd round my father to congratulate him and I was inadvertently pushed into a swarm of arms and legs. My uncle, acting as the host, led the crowd to see the rest of the house. There was plenty of laughter and shouts of admiration. Amidst all this confusion, my aunt, escaping from the company of the men, took the ladies upstairs.

With great excitement, I climbed the green-carpeted stairs. I had never seen such a thing before. As we reached the top, I was amazed at the sight before my eyes. There were huge bunches of glittering flowers of glass, or so it seemed to me, which hung from the green and gold ceiling and there were also long sofas and deep armchairs, things I had never seen before. Everything was so new and exciting that I felt an irresistible urge to touch all of them. I ran my fingers over the velvet and satin upholstery, I sat in the soft armchair, crying out elatedly when it made me bounce up and down. I did not know there were springs. I was stopped by a nasty pinch on the ear from my mother. A youth of about 19 who was standing nearby saw the pout on my face, and took me protectively by the arm. Then the tall lady with the Chinese clothes said with a smile: 'This is *Ko-Ko* (elder brother),' and pointing to two girls, added, 'these are your sisters.' I addressed them as instructed. Then my mother told me to call the tall lady *Memeh* (mother). Though I obeyed, I wondered at the same time, why I had to call her 'mother' and not 'aunt' like all the other ladies who came to visit.

Ancestral Hall of the Big House.

As Elder Brother and the two girls drew me along, I was again lost in the splendour around me. Hand in hand, the four of us roamed about, walking carefully on the lacquered floors. There were so many things I had never seen before and I plagued Elder Brother with incessant questions to which he always seemed to have an answer. Suddenly, we were in a hall where a big painting hung behind an altar.

'Look,' said Elder Brother, 'that man with the long black beard, sitting in the centre is Kwan Ti. The man with red whiskers and hair, standing on his left is Chou Ch'ang and the handsome young man on his right is Kwan Ping, his son.'

I gazed up at Elder Brother disbelievingly.

'How do you know?'

'My teacher told me.' he answered, 'Kwan Ti is the God of War and represents chivalry and bravery.'

This was beyond my comprehension and, refraining from asking more questions, I said with awe: 'The man with curly hair and whiskers and those big round eyes looks very fierce: he must be angry. Let's go away.'

Elder Brother and the sisters laughed.

We continued our exploration and came to the bedrooms. I gasped at the enormous beds with gilt fittings and white mosquitonets trimmed with ribbons and lace.

Elder Brother told me that my little brother and I were going to sleep here with my mother and he and the two girls would sleep on the other side of the house with *Memeh*. So, they were going to stay here too, I thought. They must be relatives from China who had not got a house of their own yet. Well, our house was certainly big enough for even more people than the four of them.

My little mind was too muddled to retain all that I had seen and learned in that one night. I began to feel very tired and sleepy. I cannot remember who took me to bed.

5

Mother runs away from home

THE MEMORIES I retain of *Memeh*, Elder Brother and the two sisters, are neither distant nor vague. I recall that we took our meals together at a big round table and Elder Brother taught me how to use chopsticks.

Memeh always chose the tender part of the chicken to put in my bowl of rice, and when there was something special, I was given the biggest share of it. There was a happy atmosphere as my mother and *Memeh* chatted and joked. I wished that *Memeh* and her children would always remain with us.

Sometimes, *Memeh* would take me to bed with her. She would tell me stories about fairies, queens and princesses who lived in palaces and in between, she stuffed me with candies. I found those occasions a great treat and thus became very attached to *Memeh*, seeking her more than my mother who had no time to bother about me. She was much too engrossed in looking after my little brother, who was just learning to walk. I saw very little of my father who had his meals late and alone in his private quarters in the right wing of the house. Sometimes, I was allowed to accompany him to the gate when he went to his office which was across the street.

Elder Brother took me with him whenever he went out in a rickshaw and let me enjoy the ride as long as I wanted. We would drive around the busy part of the town, across the railway line, where only the Chinese and those who had their businesses there lived.

On our way home, we usually stopped at the druggist's where they sold Chinese herbal medicine and also all sorts of Chinese sweets like plums, apricots, and pears, dried and preserved in sugar. Knowing this, the sisters, who had to stay home, were always at the door when they heard the tinkling of the rickshaw, waiting impatiently to unburden me of the various packages which I was happy to share with them. Elder Brother was very good to me and acted like a real big brother. Little did I know that he really was. Often in the evening he would take me to our father's office to fetch him home for dinner. Then my father would open a big safe from where he would take a silver dollar and give it to me. Hand in hand, the three of us would come home together.

Though Elder Brother was very protective and kind, he was too big to play games with me. He seemed to me like a hero in the old time stories. I had more fun with the sisters, running up and down stairs and slipping in and out of rooms playing hide-and-seek. I don't know how long we lived together, perhaps a few months or a year, but somehow there came a sudden end to those happy days.

It happened one night. I was already asleep when I was suddenly awakened by loud voices. My mother was shouting across the passage of the Hall of Kwan Ti at *Memeh* on the other side. I did not understand what they were shouting about, I knew only that they were not talking in their usual friendly way.

'If you dare come over here, you'll meet with my knife,' I heard my mother threaten.

Memeh's voice was subdued, but nevertheless more angry words were exchanged so rapidly that they were completely lost to me. They must be quarrelling, I thought, but why?

Suddenly, my mother burst into the little room where my little brother and I were sleeping. I sat up in bed, terribly frightened. Furiously, my mother told me to get out of bed and, throwing a jacket to me, told me to put it over my pyjamas. Then she picked up my little brother carefully so as not to awaken him and called out to our young Chinese maid, but the latter seemed to have vanished.

With a jerk, my mother pulled me along the corridor and we went down the backstairs. Leaving the house through a side door, we made for the front gate. The road was deserted. I was so confused and scared that I started to sob; my mother stopped me with a hard slap on my head. Just at this moment, a small wooden carriage drawn by a tiny *batak* horse passed by. My mother hailed it and after explaining where she wanted to go, helped me climb into the barrel-like vehicle.

Though the carriage was jostling and shaking, I soon fell asleep. When I opened my eyes again, I was aware that we had arrived at a strange house not at all like ours. A bright moon shone above us, rending the night less frightening. My mother got down first, carrying my little brother. Then I heard excited voices in the house and a door was opened. Several people came out and a woman exclaimed in a not too amiable tone: 'Well, well, what's the idea of coming home in the middle of the night and in a hired carriage too.'

My mother muttered something in response and then I was hauled out by someone and carried into the house. We found ourselves in a hall lit by a big oil lamp hanging from the wooden ceiling.

'Call *Apoh* (grandmother),' my mother told me, taking me to a middle-aged lady with a somewhat dark complexion but nevertheless very good-looking.

'*Apoh*,' I said in a very small voice.

'Hm, you've grown big since I saw you last.'

To my dismay, I could not recall having seen her before. Presently, a bulk of a man appeared in the doorway and stared at us in obvious surprise.

'This is *Akung* (grandfather),' my mother said. I shrank back and hid behind my mother. My grandfather roared with laughter. This was my first recollection of my maternal grandparents Lim and their home where I was to spend such unforgettable days.

I was rather baffled when I woke up in the morning to find myself in completely strange surroundings, a wooden house with an attap roof in the middle of a tobacco plantation. I tried to remember how we happened to be here. Then the previous night's scenes came to my mind. My mother had run away from home taking us, her children, with her.

Maternal grandfather Lim Sam-hap.

6

Mother returns in triumph

FOR A LITTLE girl of five, everything new was exciting and inspiring. I enjoyed my new environment and found it immensely interesting; especially when I found a playmate in my uncle, my mother's youngest brother who was only a few years older than I.

My little brother toddled along with us and sometimes we put him in an improvised car, a wooden case on wheels, drawn by a white goat. But when we went exploring in the forest behind the house, we left him in the care of the *singkeh* (newcomer from China) water-carrier who doted on him.

We went fishing in a shallow river and caught little fishes and shrimps, but once we caught a big carp which we brought home for my mother's younger sister to fry. We chased butterflies and although forbidden by grandmother, my uncle climbed tall trees to look for birds' eggs for me.

We were allowed to go everywhere around the plantation except the tobacco fields. All day in the open air, as free as a bird in the sky! Almost every day, we passed the shop where they sold sweet dried plums and all sorts of candies and chocolate. There was a quantity of Dutch biscuits, ham, sausages and even canned food, but those were bought only by the Dutch manager and their assistants. My uncle and I took only the sweets which the shop owner could not refuse the overseer's son.

'Never mind, take them,' and pinching my cheek, he would say: 'As for you, little girl, I'll ask your father to pay.'

One day, I came home with my hair, so neatly done in the morning by my aunt, tumbling down my flushed cheeks and my clothes wet with perspiration.

'Look,' cried my aunt in disgust and horror. She had complained more than once about my untidiness to my mother.

'Come here,' ordered my mother and without much ado, gave me strokes with the *rotan*. 'If you don't stop running about like a wild horse and losing your hairpins, I shall tie your hair with wire the next time,' she scolded.

I was too happy to care much about scoldings and the *rotan*. Neither did I miss our big and beautiful home nor *Memeh*, Elder Brother and the sisters. I seemed to have completely forgotten them. My life in the open and wild country without walls and bars, so different from life in a town, had dimmed the memory of everything in the luxurious town house. It was an exhilarating freedom which had to come to an end...

It was only later, when I was old enough, that my mother related the story about that memorable night of her flight from the Big House to her parent's house in the country. She had quarrelled with *Memeh* over a remark the latter had made during dinner. My mother was still eating when *Memeh* called her a dog and, throwing a bone to her, had said: 'Here, you dog, eat this.'

Immediately, my mother stood up, threw down her ricebowl and chopsticks and left the table. Later upstairs, *Memeh* had tried to pacify my mother explaining that she did not mean to insult her, but my mother was adamant. She had already left the house with us when my father came home from dining in the club with my uncle.

As soon as we arrived at my grandfather's home, he had sent a message to my father, informing him that we were at his home and that he was not to worry. Everything would be straightened out the next day, my grandfather had assured my father.

My father came to my grandfather's office the following morning with apologies for the inconvenience caused to his parents-in-law. He had come to take us home. To his great surprise, however, my mother refused to see him or even talk to him. My grandfather, knowing his belligerent daughter, advised my father to let the storm pass and go home alone.

After that, there were negotiations upon negotiations between grandfather and my father without any result; my mother obstinately refused to reconcile. Her rebellion left the two men, one an authority in control of the whole Chinese population and the other, a man with iron fists who was used to quelling riots among thousands of coolies single-handedly, absolutely helpless and feeling defeated.

Months passed before my mother gave her ultimatum. Unless *Memeh* and her children went back to China for good, she would never go back to my father. After much thought and a long talk with my uncle, my father gave in to my mother; and as soon as there was a boat leaving for Swatow, *Memeh*, Elder Brother and the two sisters were put on it. It was then, that I knew that *Memeh* was Mother Lee, my father's village wife. Elder Brother and the two girls were his children borne by Mother Chew.

When they had gone, my father came to fetch us in the landau drawn by a pair of white horses, the official conveyance for special occasions like going to receptions at the Sultan's palace or the Residency. The coachman was in formal livery: black coat and pants with trimming, a red waistband and a smart hat in black and red. My father's personal bodyguard in the uniform of a sergeant with decorations on his breast, stood at attention when we walked to the carriage.

My father and mother sat side by side and my little brother and I sat facing them. So, in great pomp, we returned to our mansion where my uncle and aunt were waiting in the hall to welcome us home. It was a triumph for my mother. From that moment on she was, and remained, sole mistress of the mansion until her death.

'You didn't imagine that I would come sneaking through the back door, did you? I went out through the back, but I came in only through the front,' she finished, her voice still ringing with pride. From then on she resented all Chinese women from the village.

I was never to see *Memeh* and Elder Brother again, but the two half-sisters later came back into my life.

7

The miracles of life

SINCE HIS BIRTH, my little brother Fa-liong had been a problem to my mother. He seemed always to be ailing. If it was not his stomach, it was cutting his first tooth which, for an ordinary baby, would have been quite normal, but in his case it was accompanied by spells of fever and fits.

There he was, just recovered from measles which left him coughing and choking. A Chinese *sinseh* was called. After feeling his pulse, the *sinseh* could not find anything wrong with him, but he prescribed two doses of herbal medicine to be brewed in boiling water. Then my little brother was given the black and bitter liquid which he spluttered onto his clothes. The second dose was also wasted and my little brother remained as before.

Then Grandmother Lim, who had come for a visit, suggested a *dukun* (native medical man) who was summoned from the *kampong* (village). The *dukun* scrutinised my little brother through halfclosed eyes for a long time, then declared that the boy was bewitched. He had offended a deity by urinating under an old banyan tree. My mother wondered where he could have done that and suddenly remembered that it was at my grandfather's house at the time we were staying there. My mother begged the *dukun* to cure my little brother.

My mother, with my brother on her lap, Grandmother Lim and I sat on the wooden floor in a vacant room upstairs. We watched intensely the movements of the *dukun* who sat cross-legged and with folded hands on a square mat. In front of him was placed an earthen pot filled with water, which he had fetched from the river.

Incense was burning. The old man mumbled his prayers in a monotonous chant and from time to time passed the incense over the pot. His actions were slow and the prayers interminable. I grew restless and my legs became numb, making me shift about. This irritated my mother. She glared at me. At last the old man's voice trailed to a stop. He told my father, in the same flat tone, to bathe my little brother the first thing the next morning with the water from the earthen pot where he had strewn a few flowers. My mother thanked him and slipped two green banknotes under the incense container.

The next morning, my little brother had his bath as directed by the *dukun*; first his head, then his body, and finally his hands and feet. However, he did not improve; my little brother continued to have his spasms.

Then, in despair, my father decided to consult the spirits. A medium was summoned from the temple of Kwan Ti to perform the rites.

I remember peeping through the half-closed door of the room where the session was in progress. A table was arranged like an altar with burning joss sticks, candles and offerings. Amidst the various things, I saw a pile of yellow papers with strange characters. A long sabre was laid on the right side of the table at which sat a man with closed eyes.

He was dressed in a red silk garment, tied at the waist with a broad black silk sash and a red strip of cloth was wound round his head. He was so quiet that I thought he was asleep. My father stood attentively on one side of the table and my mother, carrying my little brother in her arms, on the other side. Suddenly, the medium stirred. After several convulsive movements, he stood up with one leg on the chair. As my father and my mother watched breathlessly, the man took the sabre from the table, slapped it three times noisily on the table, then passed it quickly over his tongue. He took one of the yellow papers, snatched up a brush, put it over his bleeding tongue and wrote with the blood...

With a shriek I fled, not daring to see any more. I lay trembling in bed, and cried myself to sleep.

The next day, I heard my mother telling my aunt who had come to inquire about my brother, that the spirit of Kwan Ti had entered the body of the medium and had given *fu* (the yellow paper drawn with incantations for curing illnesses). The *fu* was burned and the ashes, mixed with water, was given to my little brother to drink.

It was a miracle. From then on my little brother was cured of his fits. As for me, I could never ever see blood again without feeling faint or ill.

8

Mother learns to read and write

IT WAS TIME for me to go to school. I was already seven. My father decided that I should go to the Dutch School. He made a request to the Resident for my admission to the government primary school hitherto exclusively reserved for Dutch children. My father's request was granted as a special favour.

Not wanting to seem ignorant, my mother sought advice from the judge's wife, who had befriended her, as to how I was to dress. So, under the supervision of this kind lady, I was outfitted with a complete set of strange garments: lace-edged white cotton pantaloons reaching to the knees, frilled cotton petticoats and short-sleeved dresses which came to just below the knees, exposing bare arms and legs; they were very different from the Chinese and native clothes I had worn up till then.

My father took me to school on the first day. I did not speak a word of the language but, because of my age, I was immediately admitted to the second class. The teacher told my father that I had to take private lessons at home in order to be able to follow the lessons. My father, who had never taken orders from anyone, conceded without protest; he was willing to do anything for his daughter's education.

My mother saw to it that I was always neatly dressed in school and, when invited to a party, I had the prettiest frock of all. Even the ribbons in my hair were always new and pressed. She spared no expenses: it was her ambition that I was neither to look nor to feel inferior to the Dutch girls. This, she did not have to worry about. With my easy-going character, I was soon taken up in their midst and treated as one of them. I was well aware that being the daughter of Tjong A Fie had a magic touch all around. And so the days of my Dutch education began.

My mother was always sitting near by when I did my homework or had my private lessons, slowly chewing her *sirih* (betel nut) and looking very severe. Though she did not understand a thing, she considered it her duty to watch over my studies. She fully comprehended that without a proper education, the Chinese could never be equal to the foreigners. My first year at school passed quite satisfactorily and so, my mother, advised by my aunt, sent me to learn Chinese from San-jin, my uncle's eldest daughter by his village wife. San-jin had recently arrived from China with her scholar husband. Thus, every afternoon after lunch, I went to my uncle's house for two hours of Chinese lessons.

We recited the Book of Confucius, Book of Verse, Book of History and the Tang poems without grasping much of the real meaning of what we learnt by rote. The philosophy of Chinese literature was too complex for our young minds. After the lesson, I was usually treated by my aunt to tea and delicious cakes before going home. The few years of Chinese lessons were thus, most enjoyable.

Cousin San-jin and husband Tsi Kun-kok.

After the Chinese lessons, I did my homework until supper time. Then, afterwards, for an hour or so, I had to learn English from my uncle Chooi-lye, my mother's younger brother who had come to stay with us because he was studying in the Pykett English School in Medan. In English, I failed badly.

Uncle Chooi-lye was a sulky and impatient young man of twenty who always scolded me for one thing or another, often making me cry. He would then complain to my mother that I was lazy and that I did not want to study. As this happened too frequently, my mother got extremely irritated.

Once, when Uncle Chooi-lye brought me again before my mother sobbing and sniffing, she thrust me aside with such violence that her heavy gold bangle hit my left cheek. I was so frightened that I did not even feel pain, but the next morning, half of my face had become purple and blue and I could not go to school for several days. My mother's remorse was so deep that she pulled off her bangles and never wore them again.

She might have hit my temple and killed me, she said. From then on, my English lessons were to my great relief suspended.

While I was progressing in my studies, my mother was contemplating her own education which she never had. She took lessons in Dutch from a lady teacher and within a year could make herself understood in that language. That was the first step towards her ambition. She also learned to write and sometimes I saw her answering a message from a Dutch lady conveyed on a slate. She read fairy tales in the beginning, but was soon absorbed in more complicated issues like social etiquette. She wanted to speak and behave as gracefully as the foreign ladies. She did not imitate, but had a natural talent for adapting. After she had acquired these social assets, she began to consider her appearance.

Though the *sarong* and *kebaya* became her very well and gave her the opportunity to wear her beautiful jewellery, she had Western clothes made which she wore at functions where foreigners were present. In her position as the wife of a leading figure in the Chinese community, she had to keep a certain dignity worthy of him. She wanted to be received in the foreign

Author's mother.   Author and Fa-liong, aged 12 and 8.

community as an equal, not as a curiosity without a personality. She wanted to be accepted in her own right and not only for her husband's wealth. For any other woman born and bred in the compound of a tobacco plantation to cope with a world unknown to her only a decade ago would be devastating. Not so with my mother: she was a born revolutionary.

Her taste in clothes was exceptional, no matter what she wore. Everytime she appeared at a function, she knew what to wear and what jewellery would match. She never looked gaudy or over dressed.

She was outstanding among the wives of the elite. Though the women would throw furtive glances of envy, the men could not deny that the Chinese lady looked exquisite. Who would have recognised the former country girl in the beautiful woman, and believed that such a transformation was possible'!

Once, my father told my mother that everybody was singing her praise to him.

'You ought to be proud of yourself. Haven't I done all this for your sake'!' my mother retorted.

When I began to take piano lessons from maestro Paci, my mother took lessons in singing from Madame Paci who was a professional singer. Madame Paci discovered that my mother was a soprano. I have heard my mother singing in intimate gatherings at our home where she was enthusiastically applauded, not out of sheer politeness, but from genuine admiration for her unusual gift and courage. It was a pity that my mother gave up singing after the Pacis left Medan.

I was about ten years old when we received the bad news that *Memeh* had passed away and, a week later, that Elder Brother had died of tuberculosis. Later I was told that the real reason for his death was that he had failed the Imperial Examinations in spite of his assiduous studies. He had been disappointed and had felt so humiliated that he had given up hope altogether, fallen ill and never got well again. He had married only the year before and left behind a widow and a son.

My mother held no grudge against *Memeh*. She said that as children had nothing to do with their elder's action, my little brother and I were to wear mourning clothes for *Memeh*. So for twelve months I wore only white and blue dresses and my long tresses were tied with blue ribbons. My little brother had his pig-tail tied with blue silk thread.

9

Aunt Liu lectures on feminine virtues

ONE DAY, MY little brother and I had the chicken pox simultaneously. As my mother was then in the family way and became unwell at the slightest provocation, my aunt offered to look after us. Besides, my father, afraid that my mother would be infected, had sent her to our country house in Poeloe Brayan and had stayed with her there. So we were left with our aunt and Nenek Botak, our native maid, in the huge house.

I shall always remember Aunt Liu who, though used to a luxurious life, abandoned her comforts to look after two sick children. I would not describe myself to be as spoiled as my brother, but in this case, we were equally trying.

Why my aunt had taken up the task of nursing us, I never understood. Was it her sense of duty towards the family, counting herself as an elder, or was it her sincere affection for us'!

Anyway, there she was, saddled with two whimpering, feverish brats; she, who never had children of her own, had to learn in her middle age about their temperament.

When my fever subsided, my brother's went sky-high. She divided her time between the two of us day and night. When I think of it now, I wonder at her stamina: anyone else in her place would have collapsed after the first week of nursing. It must have been her resilient character that kept her going.

One night, for no reason at all, we did not want to sleep on the beds in the screened-off portion of the spacious room where no mosquitoes could enter. We wanted to sleep on the floor near the window. Mattresses and pillows were carried down from the beds to the wooden floor. Patiently, Aunt Liu sat by us, chasing away the pestering insects with a fan made of palm leaves. She did not scold us for our childishness nor complain to my father when he came to see us in the morning.

Night after night, she stayed awake, reading a book, long after we were already asleep. No sooner had she picked her book up my brother would cry claiming he was thirsty. At once, Aunt Liu would be on her feet, off to pour him a cup of tea. When he was soothed, audible groans would draw her attention to me. I was sniffling and scratching all over. Aunt Liu stroked me with her soft silky fingers, telling me not to scratch my face or I would become pock-marked and nobody would want to marry me when I grew up. Those three weeks Aunt Liu looked after us, I can neither forget, nor ever repay...

I was too young to remember Aunt Liu at the time we stayed at her house, but have a better recollection of her in later days when I went to her house for my Chinese lessons. She was not a beauty, but in her thirties she was a very handsome and aristocratic-looking lady. Her face was oval with a high intelligent forehead, stern black eyes, straight nose and thin lips above a determined chin. Her skin was the colour of ivory, as if it had never been exposed on the sun. In fact it had not, for when Aunt Liu went out, it was in a carriage with closed shutters. She was sedate in all her movements and as she sat there in a straight-backed rocking chair, with one hand holding a book and the other, a straw fan, she looked like a native queen, because she always wore a *sarong kebaya*. She had an uncontestable authority about her and when she did not smile, her severity would make people wish they were miles away.

I had heard stories about Aunt Liu's *mariage de convenance* to my uncle. Aunt Liu's father, who was Chief of the Chinese in Pontianak, had sought contact with all the Chinese Chiefs in the Dutch colony to secure their positions against the Dutch. Generally family-minded, nothing could be more binding to the Chinese than two families united by marriage. Although Major Liu knew that my uncle Yong-hian had already a wife

From left to right: Author's mother. cousin San-jin and Aunt Liu.

Uncle Yong-hian with his bodyguard.

in the village, he was willing to give his daughter's hand in marriage to my uncle for the sake of mutual interests.

Aunt Liu was well read in the Chinese classics. My mother was forever grateful to her for having taught her so much since she became my father's wife, a young girl of 16, as innocent as she was ignorant.

This highly cultured elder sister-in-law had made it her business to instruct my mother in ancient traditions and customs observed by our forefathers. She read to my mother the story of *The Three Kingdoms* where loyalty and chivalry were portrayed. She told her about a woman's virtues and of filial piety. She explained Confucius' maxims and the teachings of Buddha. She also emphasised that husband and wife were to treat each other with deference and respect. How much my mother retained of all this wisdom I do not know. In later years I was well aware though, that whenever there was a quarrel between my parents, it was always my father who laid down arms first.

In spite of my mother's belligerent character, she knew how to win my aunt's affection. Both of them had outstanding inclinations which worked admirably together. As aggressive as my mother could be towards others, she was docile where it concerned Aunt Liu in whom she recognised someone dependable and who could give good advice. Aunt Liu never went out without my mother, whether it was for prayers at the temple or for a drive around town.

Aunt Liu's patience and tolerance were commendable. My uncle Yong-hian was a very handsome man, tall and fair with slender hands and fingers, a veritable aristocrat. He was soft spoken and full of dignity, so that he won admiration not only from his own but from the opposite sex as well.

Among her many virtues, Aunt Liu also taught my mother: 'We women have to tolerate our husbands otherwise the marriage will end in failure. When a wife always quarrels with the husband, there is no peace in the house and a house without peace is misfortune.'

My mother was silent; she could not decide whether or not to agree.

Aunt Liu never accompanied my uncle to any function, she disliked the idea of showing intimacy in public as the foreign ladies did. Abiding by her centuries-old customs, she considered all that foreign, barbaric and below her dignity.

She was haughty because of her upbringing but she had a generous heart. She was always the one to give and she expected nothing in return. She had an inflexible will of her own, never letting other people's opinion divert her. Being childless, she had adopted the two children, a girl and a boy, of my uncle's concubine who had died of tuberculosis.

She tolerated the presence of her step-daughter and the daughter's husband in her house although my uncle's village wife had never recognised Aunt Liu as her equal.

10

The most welcome male descendant

GRANDMOTHER LIM HAD come to stay with us while waiting for the arrival of the new baby. She did not like the idea of my mother having a doctor deliver her baby.

'Are you not ashamed,' she said to my mother, 'to expose yourself to a male person? The old *bidan* (native midwife) can do it just as well. Didn't she deliver your first three children'?' She turned up her nose and sniffed with disgust.

'But Ma, that was ten years ago,' my mother laughed. 'Your son-in-law believes in doctors now and since I haven't given birth for such a long time, he thinks I need some special attention.'

'Rubbish! A birth is the same to every woman. Your husband is influenced by the white people. He didn't object to a *bidan* before. Well, it's his money but don't expect me to stand by while the doctor is there. I wouldn't know where to hide my face,' she finished disapprovingly.

My mother just laughed. She knew that it was useless to make grandmother change her old-fashioned ideas.

A few days later, when the doctor was busy inside the room, grandmother sat outside by the door, chewing her *sirih* nervously.

My little brother and I were sent to play in the backyard.

Not long after, we heard a baby's cry.

'A boy,' we heard the doctor say to my grandmother, sticking his head through the door.

At once, there was a lot of activity in the house. The doctor came out from the room to congratulate my father who had been pacing to and fro for hours, or so it seemed to me. I saw a broad smile on my father's face as he hurried to the ancestral hall where my aunt was already preparing the necessary offerings for prayers to the God of Heaven and the ancestors for the happy event.

'My sister-in-law, the first son to be born in this house!' my father said, with tears in his eyes.

'Congratulations, my brother-in-law. I am sure your elder brother will be most happy and pleased.'

In a matter of hours the whole town knew about the new baby. The Chinese community rejoiced with my father on this most welcome male descendant. He was especially welcome because we had just lost our half-brother Kong-liang (Elder Brother).

According to custom, the birth of a baby was only celebrated when he was one month old. Presents started to pour in from the rich Chinese merchants — gold ornaments in the form of the auspicious unicorn, dragon and lion attached to heavy gold chains. There were dozens of bracelets with bells which gave a pure tinkling sound at the slightest movement.

The Sultan gave a miniature model of his palace laid out in a gleaming glass case on a stand. Every detail, like the chairs, tables, lamps and even the trees and flowers in the garden, was set with pieces of rough diamonds. It was a beautiful and unique present.

The foreigners sent typical European items like silver plates, bowls with matching forks and spoons, and a baby's wardrobe of the finest fabric and lace, made by the Dutch ladies themselves. I was old enough to admire all the beautiful things we received from people of different nationalities, including Arabs and Indians who gave gold ornaments in their style. It was a real exhibition!

Grandfather Lim, who usually came to our house only at New Year, made an exception this time. He showed up with a face flushed with excitement. Over six feet five with well-developed muscles, enormous arms and legs, he towered over me like a giant. At ten, I reached but to his stomach. He carried a big ebony stick with savvy. One would wish to be out of his way rather than in.

He greeted my father from the front door in his boisterous voice, 'Congratulations, lieutenant!' Grandfather Lim never forgot the fact that my father, though his son-in-law, was also his superior. Therefore, he preferred to address my father by his title.

Grandfather Lim was an expert in the martial arts. His forefathers were descendants from warriors. Every coolie who came to work under him knew that Lim Sam-hap was not to be trifled with. He could overpower a dozen men with his bare fists and often, in his youth, when coolies were still unruly, stopped riots singlehandedly while his Dutch superiors remained in their houses.

Grandfather Lim, with a couple of thousand sturdy and undauntable Southern Chinese under his supervision, had earned his job as overseer through years of hardship, bravery and integrity. Whatever the circumstances, his courage never failed him. He was the only Chinese overseer who was decorated by the Dutch government for his valuable services.

Grandfather Lim brought with him a gold *Chi Ling*, the auspicious unicorn, for his new-born grandson. After letting him admire the baby, my father entertained him with a cockerel cooked in wine and stewed pork leg which he easily finished by himself. After having downed a bottle of brandy between them, grandfather went back to his estate. His parting caress for me was a pat on my head which made me reel in its force.

Undoubtedly, this little third brother Kian-liong was the luckiest of us all because he was born at the pinnacle of my father's success.

11

Tragedy at Poeloe Brayan

THE FIRST AND best friend of my school days was Elly Kruseman, the judge's daughter, whose mother taught Mama how to dress me. Elly was my age, and had dark brown hair with a slight wave in it. Her eyes were a mixture of light grey and green with dark brown curly lashes.

Her elder sister Winnie was a very beautiful girl of sixteen but extremely haughty. She looked condescendingly on the boys who tried to win her favour and when they addressed her, she simply turned her back on them.

Every Sunday, I was asked to the Krusemans' to play and at the same time to profit from the home education the girls were given. I must say that I have much to thank Aunt Kruseman for my basic foreign education which in the course of my life, with all the changes, remained useful to me. Thus Elly and I became inseparable friends; wherever she went I was also invited and we confided in each other our little secrets and our likes and dislikes of persons and things.

One day, we gave a childrens' party at our country house in Poeloe Brayan where we had a zoo.

Over fifty children were invited together with their parents who enjoyed themselves just as much. We visited the monkeys, orang-utans, big parrots, tiny parakeets, white cockatoos, peacocks, clucking turkeys, singing canaries, guinea pigs, fleck less rabbits and a huge python locked in a separate cage.

At the back of the garden, in vast open enclosures, were the cassowaries, giraffes, zebras and a grey donkey. Among them hopped the kangaroos; one of them even had a baby kangaroo peering out from its pouch. It was great fun.

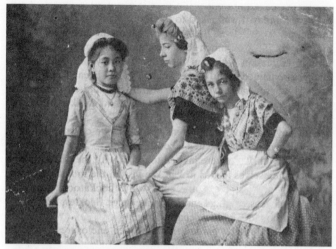

Author with friends Winnie and Elly Kruseman dressed as Dutch peasants.

Author, going to a carnival with friends, in a decorated car
in front of the Big House in Medan.

The bigger boys climbed the rambutan and mangosteen trees. They threw the fruits to the girls who waited eagerly below with outstretched hands and some more enthusiastic ones held up their dresses to receive their share. It was a real plunder; but my father just laughed. He only warned us all not to go near the lake which was in a more isolated section of the estate.

We had an enormous lunch in the garden, sitting on mats laid out on the soft grass. After the heavy meal, some of us sprawled lazily on the grass while others went to feed the monkeys with the leftover food. The adults were in the house chatting over their cups of coffee or mugs of beer. It had been a lovely day and we all decided to return to Medan after four when the day was cooler.

All of a sudden, we were alerted by two boys, sons of the Garrison-Major, who came running to the house to report that their friend Broer Bleckman, the Colonel's son, had disappeared in the lake. On hearing this, Mrs. Bleckman screamed and ran wildly to the lake, followed by the men. Those who remained behind tried to control the panic the news had brought. Girls cried hysterically. Unfortunately, the Colonel was on an expedition in Atjeh.

My father ordered the gardeners to search the lake, helped by some guests who could swim. It was a sunny day and the water had been warm and clear and had thus tempted the three boys to swim, despite my father's warning not to go near the lake.

The men waded through the water plants and reeds, poking the bottom of the lake with long bamboo poles.

After more than an hour of intense search, when the sun was already going down, Broer was found in a shallow part of the lake, covered by reeds. It was a mystery why no one had seen the body earlier. Broer was carried out of the water, a beautiful white corpse, still soft, with tightly closed eyes. Nothing could revive him any more.

Mrs. Bleckman knelt down beside her boy and kissed his forehead, saying: 'Go with God, my boy.'

Then four men lifted him and carried him to our closed carriage drawn by two black horses. Mrs. Bleckman accompanied her son in the carriage back to Medan. Who would have thought that such a joyful day would end in such a tragedy!

The next day when my mother called on her, Mrs. Bleckman, hardly able to hold back her tears, patted my mother's hand gently and said: 'Don't grieve for me. It is God's will and God shall return my son.'

12

Father meets the black sheep

OUR FIRST AUTOMOBILE was a Fiat convertible, painted
yellow with red lines all around the border: we called it '*motor
kuning*' (yellow car). A Malay chauffeur was engaged and Fa-
liong and I were impatient to ride in it. When Papa took us out
for the first time, we were terribly excited and could not stop
chattering. It ran faster than a horse-carriage and there was no
need to fear a horse bolting. How enthusiastic we were over
our motor car! We did not yet know of the inconveniences
that an automobile could cause.

I never realised how wealthy my father was until he told my
mother one day that he had bought a rubber estate. And one
Sunday, he took us to see it. Papa and Mama had little Kian-
liong between them and Fa-liong and I sat on the two flapping
seats, while the old *nenek* was in front with the driver and a
boy attendant.

We started early, going along places I had never seen before.
We passed a tobacco plantation called Tandjong Merawa,
then came to Lubu Pakan, a town where the population was
mostly Chinese with a chief named Lieutenant Liao. The
next town was called Simpang Tiga, domain of the Sultan of
Sendang, a friend of Papa's. We stopped here for a while to see
his specimen of an orang utan. The further we proceeded the
more interesting the country became. At last after a drive of
three hours we turned into a private road where a signboard
indicated 'Si Boelan'.

The manager of the estate, a stout Dutchman, waited for
us at the foot of the stairs of his thatched wooden bungalow.
Mr. Kamerlingh Onnes greeted my parents with respect and

helped my mother up the wooden steps. He invited Papa and Mama to sit down in the big rattan armchairs and ordered a Javanese boy to serve coffee and snacks. We children were given lemonade. After the refreshments, Papa said that he wanted to make the rounds of the estate with the manager.

I was later to learn that my father had met Mr. Kamerlingh Onnes when the latter was out of a job. He was the 'black sheep' of a well-known and respected family in Holland, but owing to circumstances, had been sent to the East Indies to become a planter. However his hot temper caused him to be dismissed from more than one job. So sitting alone in the Medan Hotel with an empty glass before him, he had been meditating on his next move when my father approached the solitary man. The sight of his torn clothes and his frayed canvas shoes aroused my father's curiosity because he had never seen a white man in such a pitiful state. Hearing his plight, my father, convinced of his honesty, offered him a job as manager of his newly acquired rubber estate — an offer which the man accepted at once. Both never regretted this strange meeting. Mr. Onnes acquitted himself so well in his job that he won my father's full confidence and Papa never bought another estate without consulting him. They were more than employer and employee, they became staunch friends. When my father's new enterprise in rubber grew, Mr. Onnes set up an administrative office, handling my father's interests.

The former 'black sheep' had done credit to his family. He was chief inspector of all my father's rubber, coconut and tea plantations. During my father's lifetime this friend's loyalty never wavered.

My father was the first Chinese to own rubber estates and employ white men to work for him. So, Tjong Sui-fa's prediction that the young man with the bronze face was to have position, wealth and power had come true. I was too young then to know the power of money and its never failing magic. That my father had gone through hardships, I could not picture. I did not realize that he had had to dig and sweat before the tree he planted grew bigger and bore fruit.

When my father and Mr. Onnes came back from their inspection, with flushed faces and their clothes soaked in perspiration, I watched them taking off their topees and wiping their sweat from their foreheads.

Looking down at my upturned face, my father asked me how I liked it there.

'It's a very big estate, isn't it Papa? You must have walked a long way.'

'Yes, my little girl and if we are lucky, Papa will buy you a nice present,' answered my father.

'You see, Mr. Onnes,' my mother chipped in, 'he's always spoiling his daughter.'

'If she were mine, I would do the same,' laughed the manager, patting my cheek with his fat hand.

'What do you say to a trip to Penang?' my father asked my mother.

'And the children? Who's going to look after them?' my mother hesitated.

'Take all of them along and old Nenek too,' said my father generously.

My mother smiled at him alluringly, knowing she had won him over completely, but said: 'I really don't want to go.'

'Ladies always say things that are contrary to what they think,' put in Uncle Onnes with a chuckle.

After lunch, the men went to work in the office until four o'clock and then came back for tea. They seemed satisfied with the results of the day. After taking the lavishly prepared tea, we said good-bye to Uncle Onnes and thanked him for the lovely day. I will never forget my first visit to 'Si Boelan'.

13

Aunt Cheah tells her story

MY FIRST EXPERIENCE of a sea voyage was quite thrilling. At the start the wide open sea frightened me; I wondered how the captain would find his way to our destination. But soon, my attention was diverted by dolphins, which I had only seen in pictures before then, racing alongside the boat. The jellyfish intrigued me too, soft masses without heads or tails bobbing about in the waves.

The next morning after sunrise, we saw land looming before us. It was Penang with Malaya on the horizon. We clapped our hands excitedly and little Kian, who was then three and very naughty, jumped down from my mother's lap and put his head through the railings to see better, to the great consternation of old Nenek.

There was hustle and bustle everywhere. Standing at the railings, I noticed a group of *nonyas* (Chinese ladies) and a *towkay* (Chinese gentleman) coming on board. The man wore the traditional Chinese loose jacket and baggy black silk trousers. The ladies were dressed in *sarong* and *kebaya* and their hair was piled on top of their heads in chignons adorned with rows of heavy gold and diamond hair-pins, like my mother's.

The gentleman, a debonair middle-aged man with a loud voice, introduced himself as Cheah Choon-sen, relative by marriage and father-in-law of my uncle's second daughter. The three ladies were his daughters, all married and about my mother's age. Uncle Cheah extended his invitation to us to stay at his house.

Aunt Cheah, a stern-looking lady in her forties, welcomed us heartily and of course, we children were the centre of attention. Little Kian with his round mischievous eyes and the cute tuft of hair on top of his well-shorn head especially won Aunt Cheah's affection and she called him *Djamboel* (Tuft). This nickname remains with him to this day. We enjoyed our stay tremendously. We had a number of cousins to play with; we were spoilt with cakes and sweets and above everything, my mother could not grumble at us or scold us as she was too busy shopping, accompanied by the daughters of Uncle Cheah.

Uncle Cheah, besides his two overseas wives also had a very young one from Canton whom we called Aunt Number Three. She was about eighteen and very pretty. We liked her very much. Sometimes when Uncle Cheah was not at home, she would come downstairs and play with us as she loved children.

One day I watched with great curiosity Aunt Cheah smoking opium. Lying on a broad divan beside her opium set, Aunt Cheah prepared her smoke herself. Holding a pinch of the black stuff on a long needle, she heated it against the flame of a small oil lamp until it sizzled in a ball. Then she took it between her forefinger and thumb and inserted it into the hole of a long pipe, and began inhaling with an air of satisfaction and delight. I found the smell somewhat nauseating.

'He was such a bright boy and so handsome,' she said in a deep shaky voice when my mother asked why she had taken to smoking opium. 'He had just returned from London with an LL.B degree and was already engaged to be married. Every afternoon he went driving in his phaeton with the pair of chestnuts which he had brought from England. He had a splendid figure, my son; he handled his horses with such expertise. All the young girls waited at the windows just to see him pass.'

Aunt Cheah paused with a deep sigh, took a fresh smoke and continued: 'It was as if I had a presentiment. I told him not to go out that evening. He just laughed, knowing my habit of worrying every time he went driving. He did not listen to me and that was the last time I saw him alive. Some people brought his dead body home. They had seen the accident. His horses shied at a shadow and bolted. He was thrown out…' Aunt Cheah's voice trailed away in a whisper, then, as if talking to herself: 'Had he been alive today, I would be a grandmother.'

Two teardrops rolled down her face.

My mother, deeply moved, tried to say a few consoling words.

And I realised for the first time that human life was not as happy as it appeared and that material things could never compensate a broken heart.

Aunt Cheah and Third Lady Cheah.

ॐ

14

The elite of Penang

AUNT CHEAH Number Two introduced Mama to the elite of Penang. I was usually allowed to go along. We visited many places, each day a different one, such that it seemed to me like a whirlwind of excitement.

The first house we went to was the mansion of Uncle Cheah's neighbour, Tio Tiauw-set. It was a very big Chinese-style house surrounded by a red brick wall. The open courtyard was paved with polished red tiles. There were numerous porcelain pots of dahlias, chrysanthemums, roses and camellias encircling a large pond where pink and white nemophilia grew. Inside the building, the walls and ceiling were painted with colourful historic figures, dragons and phoenix.

The ancestral shrine was beautifully carved and overlaid with gold. Furniture were of ebony and rose-wood inlaid with mother-of-pearl. Cabinets displayed antique porcelain vases and bowls. In the big hall hung two big Chinese lanterns encased with glass panels with gilded frames. There was nothing foreign in the decor.

The host, an old gentleman of about sixty, tall and austere looking, waited for us in the reception hall surrounded by his concubines and slave-girls. Tio Tiauw-set was a pioneer who had become a millionaire, owning vast tin mines in Ipoh. He came to know my father when the latter arrived from China and as he saw great future in the young man with the bronze face, had become his protector and friend. As my father was a generation younger, I had to call the old man 'great-uncle' and kow tow before him and he gave me an *ang-pow* (red packet). It contained four gold coins worth ten English pounds each.

After the formalities and small talk, the old man shot a look at the slave-girl who then went about sedately to serve tea and cakes. It was customary with the mandarins that when tea was served it was a sign that the visit had come to an end so as to relieve the host of his duties of interminable entertaining. Thus when great-uncle Tiauw-set raised his cup, we all followed his example, after which we stood to bid our farewells. To my regret the cakes were not touched though they must have been as delicious as they looked. To this day his mansion stands proudly in Leith Street, Penang.

I was so confused by the many strange faces and the different things that I saw in each household that everything seemed like a dream. There were so many rich people with beautiful mansions in Penang. One family was as wealthy as the other, if not wealthier. Many of them had found their fortune in tin mining and they tried to outshine one another in the architecture of their grand homes. Each house was as luxuriously decorated as the other with gilded furniture, crystal chandeliers, Venetian glass lamps and bibelots.

One house which has remained in my memory is that of Chung Thye-phin. It was like a castle with two towers and was built on a hill. The garden stretched to the sea. Black marble steps led to a porticoed entrance with two rose-coloured marble Greek statues on either side. When we entered the big hall, my eyes were arrested by a life-size oil painting of an extremely handsome young man in a costume such as that worn by English lords: white breeches, sapphire blue long-tailed cutaway coat, frilly white shirt and a high cravat. His head was covered with a white wig, his hand poised lightly on a small table and on his little finger he wore a huge diamond ring, its unmistakable blue sparkle skillfully brought out by the artist. He held a white lace handkerchief in his left hand. He looked so elegant and grand that I could hardly take my eyes off him.

'That's the owner of this castle,' said Aunt Cheah Number Two, pointing to the picture.

At this moment, a beautiful young woman came down the stairs. She was very fair, her face a perfect oval with a straight nose and full red lips. Her eyes were bright and smiling. She was wearing a pale green gauze *kebaya* with a large floral design and a brown batik *sarong*. Her black hair was done in a style like my mother's with jasmines to adorn it and she wore exquisite jewellery.

'She has the most beautiful jewellery in all of Penang,' whispered Aunt Cheah again. Turning to the young woman who had reached the foot of the stairs to greet us, she said aloud, 'I've brought my relative from Medan to make your acquaintance and to see your house.'

'You're very kind,' Mrs. Chung acknowledged in a sweet voice, 'you are always welcome.'

She led us through the house from one room to another, each laid out differently. Then she took us upstairs to their living quarters. Her bedroom was separated from that of her husband's by a cosy drawing room and a study.

'We usually spend the evenings here because my husband likes the privacy of his study where he can read and write undisturbed while I do some embroidery,' she told us.

The bedroom was an absolute dream. The walls were panelled with *bois-de-rose* brocade which was also used for draperies for the windows over cream-coloured lace curtains. The soft sunlight shimmered through accompanied by a cool breeze from the sea. The bed was in the form of a big shell covered with a canopy decorated with silver cupids. The pillows and bedspread were of pink lace and satin. On the floor lay a fleecy cream-coloured carpet and the high ceiling was painted with lilies-of-the-valley and forget-me-nots.

Adjoining the bedroom was the dressing room. In it stood a long three sided looking glass in which one could see oneself from three angles. Along the wall, near the window, stood the dressing table arranged with big and small bottles of perfume, and in crystal containers — a variety of face powder! Noticing my curiosity, Mrs. Chung smiled sweetly and said: 'I only use *bedak sejuk* (pure rice powder), it's best for the skin.' A panelled closet contained her wardrobe of *sarongs*, *kebayas* and slippers embroidered with gold and silver threads, sequins and multi-coloured beads.

A connecting door opened to the bathroom laid with rose tiles. Even in this room everything was luxurious: sets of towels in matching colours, soaps, bathcubes and other curiosities. Seeing these, Aunt Cheah remarked: 'If I had to use all these, I'd rather go without a bath.' It made us all laugh, but I felt for the first time something like envy. To be surrounded by so much luxury and beautiful things all the time must be marvellous, I thought.

Finally, Mrs. Chung took us downstairs to have tea in the dining room built under the sea. We sat at a long table laid with all sorts of delicacies. We really enjoyed the tea and I ate to my heart's content. When I happened to look up at the ceiling I saw that it was not painted as I had at first thought. It was a glass dome through which I could see fishes swimming about!

Seeing my astonishment, Mrs. Chung explained amiably: 'Yes, they are real fishes. My husband designed this room himself and had it built under the sea. He claims that it will relieve our boredom if we have our meals in the company of fishes. It is a pity that he is now in London buying racehorses but he will be back for the Gold Cup next month. Then, he can show you more of his eccentricities.'

It was beyond my comprehension what money could bring about. I now understood how wealthy people in Penang were and that they knew how to enjoy life. After seeing all this, our big house in Medan seemed insignificant, but it was our home and we were very happy. I wondered whether all the people we had seen in their luxurious homes felt the same.

The last and most important visit for my mother was to the house of Chew in Kelawei; late Mother Chew's maiden home. My mother by marrying my father after Mother Chew's death became the daughter of the house according to ancient Chinese customs. Aunt Wu-nyong, Mother Chew's younger sister, who was a widow, took us to the family house for dinner. All the members of the household regarded my

mother as a substitute for Mother Chew and called my mother
'elder sister' though she was much younger in age.

I remember Aunt Wu-nyong vividly when she first came
to Medan. I was then about 10 years old. She was the most
beautiful Penang lady I ever saw dressed in a long gauze
kebaya and exquisite batik *sarong*. She was also the first and
only woman my father entertained socially because she was
his sister in-law, sister of his dead wife.

My mother accompanied Aunt Wu-nyong to see my father
while he was having dinner. She sat on the rattan settee facing
him and they talked about what seemed serious things. The
next day, Aunt Wu-nyong left for Penang and we did not see
her again until *Ch'ng Beng* (Tomb Sweeping Festival). This
time she came with her two sons, Hock-yong and Hock-eam.
We were about the same age and played together while Aunt
Wu-nyong went about her business.

Later I was told that Aunt Wu-nyong's husband had died in
Medan and was buried there. Her yearly visits was to pray at his
tomb and her last visit with her sons was to collect his remains
to be brought back to Penang for reburial. For decades I lost
all contact with Aunt Wu-nyong's family. It was only in 1974
that I met cousin Hock-earn and his wife when they came to
visit our house at Medan. Before returning to Medan we were
invited by Aunt Cheah Number Two to stay a few days with
her. Though her house was only a shophouse without a garden,
I had fun since I had so many girl-cousins of my age and some
older ones to play with. While my mother went shopping with
the ladies, we were left at home with Nenek and Djamboel.

On the night before our departure we were lucky enough
to see the Moon Festival celebrations. Sitting in front of the
house we watched the decorated floats pass by. Each portrayed
a scene from ancient stories and the protagonists were played
by young girls in colourful ancient array. There were kings,
queens, princesses, fairies, peasants and warriors besides those
disguised as animals, birds and fish. It was terrific! Seeing the
girls wearing a lot of jewellery, I asked Aunt Cheah whether
they were real.

Author (fourth from right) with cousin Hock-eam and family
in the Big House in 1974.

'Of course,' she answered. 'Look! That girl balancing on the
long bamboo pole is bedecked with the beautiful ornaments
of Mrs. Chung. She wants the girl to have the pleasure of
winning a prize. There are also wealthy ladies who lend their
jewellery to these girls, on guarantee by their sponsors, for this
annual event, in order to show off,'

I had seen and learnt many things in Penang which I could
not have had my father not given me the opportunity. As for
my mother, her shopping resulted in a new set of diamond
kerungsang (brooches) and *tusuk kondelz* (hairpins).

15

The brothers Tjong become a legend

MY UNCLE AND aunt had moved to their new home at Kewawan. It was in the same block as our home and was only separated by my uncle's haberdashery. At the back was a godown with a big yard where we could go in and out of both houses unobtrusively.

The first Chinese school, the Tun Pun School, was founded by my uncle and father, with cousin San-jin's husband as principal. Besides this school, the brothers Tjong had also established a foundation, the 'Tjie On Jie Jan'; a Chinese hospital, where free medical services were given, with an annexe for the aged and destitute. Coffins were donated to the poor. On Chinese New Year Day, two suits were distributed to each of the needy. The foundation was run by a committee comprising capable family members and headed by the founders themselves. They handled funds donated to Chinese temples and communal burial grounds. Thus the names Tjong Yong-hian and Tjong A Fie became legendary not only among the Chinese community but also among other nationalities because my father gave freely to churches as well as to mosques and Hindu temples.

In the days of the pioneers, the Chinese were given ample opportunities to help the Dutch build the country they ruled and as the Chinese were an assiduous and industrious race, they had become successful whether as coolies or tradesmen. That the results of my uncle's and my father's work were more far-reaching than that of their contemporaries must be attributed to their zeal, genius and most of all, luck. Though they had earned their fortunes the hard way, this did not stop them from donating great amounts wherever and whenever their goodwill was called upon. Big sums of money were sent to China to relieve victims of drought, flood or famine. Roads and bridges were built in their home village and schools set up for peasant children.

My uncle, who was more ambitious than my father, organised the Chao-chow and Swatow Railway Company near his hometown, Mei Hsien, for which he was awarded the honorary title of Minister of Railways by the Manchu Government. He was received in audience by the Empress Dowager Tse Hsi who, not failing to notice the handsome aristocrat, treated him with special attention. He was served bird's nest from Siam in a golden bowl and saucer which was afterwards presented to him as a sign of Imperial favour.

He had the distinction of the red coral button on his mandarin hat and his mandarin robes were embroidered

Uncle Yong-hian when he was president of the
Chao-chow and Swatow Railway Company.

with the dragon as worn by the Ching aristocracy. My uncle's pride was great. It was said that when he visited his village, forerunners beat on gongs to announce his arrival; villagers had to kneel by the roadside, as they would do for a special emissary of the Son of Heaven, as he passed in his red topped sedan-chair carried by eight uniformed men. He vaunted his importance in bringing glory to the village as his ancestors had done many generations back. He had a new mansion erected next to the ancestral home, as befitted his position. Unfortunately, he was not to occupy it.

Swatow Railway Currency (front and back).

Aunt Liu had been ill for some time and not wanting to worry my uncle with her illness, she moved back to the old house where she was attended to by her relatives who had come with her from Pontianak. She refused to consult a doctor and took only herbal medicines. My mother failed in persuading my aunt to see a specialist.

One day, after my Chinese lesson, my mother took me to see Aunt Liu. She was lying on a thick mattress on the wooden floor of her private apartment upstairs. Propped up by pillows, she looked very frail. Nothing was left of the impressive personality. Gone was her erect posture. Her face was pale, her mouth drawn at the corners, her chin hung loose above a neck deeply wrinkled, and her eyes were dull. Her hair was pulled back in a knot at the back of her head with only one gold pin stuck into it; normally, she wore beautiful diamond hairpins. Neither was she wearing the immense ear-knobs nor the gorgeous *kerungsang* to fasten her *kebaya* which was now held together by safety pins to cover her shrunken body. I was shocked to see the change in this once formidable aunt and could hardly bring myself to address her. My mother and I sat near her feet. She looked at me and with a shadow of a smile. said in a weak voice: 'How are you getting on with your lessons'!'

Holding back tears, I answered, nodding my head vigorously.

Then she spoke again: 'Remember that you must always obey your parents.'

I stuttered: 'Yes, my aunt.' That was the last time I saw Aunt Liu. She died of cancer of the womb.

My uncle was shattered with grief. He knew that he had lost not only a wife who had tolerated all his escapades, but a loyal friend. Leaning on her coffin, he kept calling: 'My dear wife, my loyal friend, my eternal companion.'

Aunt Liu had left all her jewellery to her two adopted children, Fo-jin and Lai-liong, and her relatives were handsomely rewarded for their devotion. Though outwardly severe, Aunt Liu had a heart of gold.

16

Tjong A Fie takes over

AT THE TIME we were blessed with another brother, Kwet-liong, my half-sister Song-jin and her husband arrived from China. She was a petite woman with a loud voice and agitated mannerisms.

Her husband was an athletic-looking young man with a quiet nature. He wore foreign clothes and had a false pig-tail.

I understood that he had studied in Japan and was a revolutionary. I did not grasp what it was all about then. My father told his son-inlaw to do away with the pig-tail because he did not approve of hypocrisy and he also warned him to refrain from unlawful activities lest he be deported.

My mother received them well, allowing them to stay in the left wing formerly occupied by Mother Lee (*Memeh*). When Aunt Wu-nyong came from Penang to see her niece, she was appreciative of my mother's generous treatment of her late sister's child. Three months later, sister Song-jin gave birth to a son.

On my fourteenth birthday, my father gave me a bicycle and of course my mother insisted that Fa-liong have one also. Every evening, in the backyard, my brother-in-law taught us how to ride. Although we suffered many bruises we had a grand time together.

Having completed my advance primary education, I had to take the high school entrance examination to determine if I was to continue my education in Holland or Batavia. As I preferred Holland, I did my best. My father was very pleased with my results and promised to let me go to Holland. However, due to unforeseen circumstances, all that had been planned did not materialize and my life completely changed its course.

My father was due for his furlough and left for a trip to China with the intention of visiting his village where a new mansion had been built for his retirement. He had just arrived in Hong Kong when a telegram called him back to Medan. My uncle had suddenly passed away.

That morning, my mother and I had gone to the Toko Dusun, a fashion store of which she was a regular customer. She and Mrs. Duson had become very good friends and the Duson children came to our house to play on Sundays. My mother was trying on a new dress when an attendant from my father's office came to tell her that my uncle had suddenly been taken ill.

We went home immediately. When my mother arrived at the office, my uncle was already beyond help. He was carried back to his house. Aunt Hsi, my uncle's village wife, who had just come from China a few months ago, was thrown into a state of despondency, the more so because of my father's absence.

My father returned a week later, but the funeral took place only after all my uncle's children had arrived from China. My uncle was buried in his private grounds in Petissa where he had built a secluded house surrounded by a vast garden through which a river ran. According to the Chinese this was an auspicious place.

Uncle Yong-hian's funeral.

The vacancy caused by my uncle's death had to be filled and my father was unanimously selected as his successor. With my father's promotion to Captain, there was a re-shuffle among the other chiefs and new nominations had to be made. The result reached was to the satisfaction of everyone involved. My father employed in this matter his sense of fair play; there was no favouritism, simply the right man for the right job at the right time.

Grandfather Lim was nominated lieutenant for the Chinese in Pangkalan Brandan, a booming petroleum town. Though people might have whispered about grandfather's nomination, in the end they had to bow to my father's good judgement because the job in Pangkalan Brandan was the most difficult and the least enviable. The Chinese in that region were mostly Hai Lok Hongs, descendants of Southern Chinese fighters

Author (standing on the right) with Uncle Kim and
his wife in their house in Medan (1970s).

and pirates, unruly and fearless; but grandfather Lim, himself a Hai Lok Hong, had them well under control.

With all these occurrences no attention was given to my further studies, and having missed the term, I had to wait another year. In the course of the year, another misfortune befell us. My grandmother Lim died of a heart attack; she was only forty-nine. My mother took her youngest brother, Uncle Kim, to stay with us in Medan and later sent him to the Pykett School in Penang.

17

Queeny meets her fate

WE CAME TO know the Pyketts of the Methodist mission in Penang when they started the first English school in Medan. My father provided the land for the school.

During their occasional visits to Sumatra, they stayed at our country house in Poeloe Brayan. Thus, in return, they invited us to spend our holidays with them. So, my mother took Fa-liong, Djamboel and me, leaving our new little brother in the care of sister Song-jin.

I was eagerly looking forward to the trip, remembering the numerous girl cousins I met three years ago. They must have grown up into young ladies. I too was no longer a skinny clumsy girl I was said to have a pleasant face despite my freckles.

The Pyketts had two one-storey wooden houses in Burmah Road which shared a vast garden and playground. Their large family lived in one and the other was set aside as a boarding house for outstation students like Uncle Kim. It was also used as a school for orphans. Besides Uncle Kim, there were three other boarders; two of them were from Medan, Wee Gim-keng and Yap Gin-sek, and one from Tjeribon, Java.

On the day of our arrival, we were invited to a lunch with about twenty other guests. We sat at a long table with a wide variety of curries, *satay* and other delicious dishes. The aroma whetted our appetites. Indian girls neatly dressed in white blouses and colourful *sarongs* served us.

I was sitting between Elizabeth and Dick Pykett whom I knew well from their visits to Medan. During the meal, they teased me by stepping on my foot or pulling at my dress under the table. I did my best to behave as a young girl should, but could not suppress a smile on a few occasions. The boy from Java, introduced to me as Tan Wan-hoei, sat facing us. He looked smilingly at me now and then, and seemed amused. I did not have the faintest idea that my mother was watching from the head of the table where she sat next to the host When lunch was over, we went upstairs where two large rooms had been reserved for us. We had hardly entered one of the rooms when my mother immediately cried out: 'Shameless girl! What is there to laugh about? Looking at and laughing at boys, attracting their attention. Did I teach you to do all this?'

Rather taken aback by this, I answered: 'I did not look at boys, I did not laugh with boys, I was only amused by Elizabeth's teasing.'

'What! You dare to say that? I saw you looking at the boy opposite you and laughing with him.'

'I did not,' I said firmly though tears were running down my face.

'Did not, did not, you still want to deny it?' my mother grumbled. 'And don't leave this room,' she continued, 'I am going to see Aunt Cheah.'

When she returned a couple of hours later, my mother announced that we were moving to Aunt Cheah's house immediately. Thinking of it now, I wonder what reason or excuse she could have given to the Pyketts for leaving their home so suddenly.

The next day, however, Elizabeth and Dick came to take us to their house for a children's party given in our honour. My mother could not refuse the invitation. We had an enjoyable time playing games with the orphans.

Later, leaving the younger children playing at their games, Elizabeth and her cousin Winnie took me upstairs to the balcony for tea. Elizabeth encouraged me to speak in English so we chatted in a mixture of that language and Malay because Winnie, who had just arrived from England, wanted to learn Malay. We shrieked with laughter at one another's mispronunciations. Our merriment must have aroused the curiosity or perhaps induced the irritation of the boys who were playing football in a field nearby. A ball came flying through the air and landed in the balcony.

'That must be George, my brother,' exclaimed Elizabeth angrily.

'We'll hide the ball so they can't play.'

Soon, we heard George shouting at the top of his voice: 'Liz, throw us the ball.'

Elizabeth shrugged her shoulders and showing her empty hands, feigned ignorance.

'Come on, silly. I saw the ball land there.'

'Did you do it purposely'!'

'Yes. You girls disturbed us with your silly laughing.'

Winnie and I remained silent, enjoying the quarrel and suppressing our giggles.

Just then, one of the boarders, the boy who sat opposite us at lunch appeared at the bottom of the stairs. He stopped and looked up hesitantly. On an impulse, I picked up the ball and threw it to him.

'Thank you,' he said with a smile.

I smiled back as he turned on his heels.

For a moment our eyes had met and in that moment our fates had crossed each other to weave the unforgettable drama of our lives. A few days later, on a Sunday afternoon, Elizabeth and Dick came to take Fa-liong and me to the cinema. We went in two rickshaws. Suddenly, I felt someone holding on to our rickshaw. I looked back and recognised the boy from Java.

'It's only Wan-hoei, don't be scared,' laughed Elizabeth. 'He's coming to the pictures too.'

I remember that it was an English movie featuring the British Royal Family. The life of the Prince of Wales was highlighted from babyhood to youth. He looked grand in his naval uniform. Elizabeth nudged me, whispering how handsome the prince was. We were both so absorbed in admiration of the King-to-be that I hardly heard what the boy sitting next to me was saying. It was Wan-hoei.

After the film, he asked me whether I would like to go to the Botanical Gardens on Sunday.

'Do come,' urged Elizabeth.

'I don't know whether my mother will give me permission.'

'Don't worry, my mother will ask her,' Elizabeth said convincingly, 'besides, it will be your last day in Penang. We must spend it together.'

Somehow, I never mentioned to my mother that Wan-hoei was also at the pictures and that he had asked me to meet him at the Botanical Gardens.

One day, my mother visited the Ayer Itam Buddhist temple (*Kek Lok Si*) built on Penang Hill. After leading us through halls filled with beautiful gilded Buddhas, the abbot, Pun-chung, took us to the top of the building where there was a pavilion with a wide terrace built with funds contributed by my father.

In a carved cabinet were life-like sculptures of the donors dressed in the Mandarin costumes of the pioneers with baggy black silk trousers and white jackets. I could recognise great-uncle Tio Tiauw-set, uncle Cheah Choon-sen, my uncle Yong-hian and my father among them. We were entertained with lavishly prepared vegetarian food.

One afternoon, Mrs. Pykett invited my mother for tea at her house to meet a very good friend of hers. I was allowed to go along. I saw a beautiful lady dressed in a Chinese jacket and pleated skirt, a fashion I had never seen before. Her hair was done in a coil and held by a single gold pin in the form of a butterfly. The lady spoke English fluently and as my mother did not speak the language, Mrs. Pykett had to interpret. Nevertheless the conversation seemed to carry on amicably. Elizabeth and I watched from a distance and I could see that my mother was rather impressed by the beautiful lady, something that seldom happened. At that time I did not have the slightest notion that we had met such an important person as Mrs. Sun Yat-sen. She was on her way to China. My mother even copied the way she dressed when we returned to Medan.

At last Sunday came. We went first to Elizabeth's house in Uncle Cheah's carriage — Fa-liong, Djamboel, old Nenek and I. We then drove to the Botanical Gardens where Wan-hoei was already waiting. I was pleased to see him and together we

Dr. & Mrs. Sun Yat-sen
(Photo courtesy of Mr. C.K. Tseng).

walked around the spacious grounds. A band was playing on
a platform. We listened to it for a while and then Wan-hoei
took us to eat ice cream and cakes. I did not feel that I was
doing something wrong in accepting Wan-hoei's invitation, as
I was not meeting him secretly, what with Elizabeth hovering
about us like a mother hen. We went up a hill where a small
waterfall flowed down to the lily pond. It was almost sunset
and the sky was changing its colours. It was beautiful. All too
soon, it was time to go home. Djamboel ran down the hill and
I followed him. Near the bottom, he fell down and I, unable
to stop, passed him, the point of my shoe hitting his cheek.
He did not cry out and I thought all was well.

Wan-hoei wished me goodbye and a pleasant voyage and
thus we parted. My mother did not suspect in the least that
I had seen Wan-hoei without her knowledge and I did not
feel guilty about hiding it from her for there was nothing
improper in our meeting.

The following day found Djamboel with a bruised cheek. I
confessed to my mother who, wonder of wonders, did not scold
but only said: 'What will your father say when he sees that?'

18

Queeny grows up

AFTER OUR RETURN from Penang no mention was made again about my going to Holland. Instead, my mother thought that it was time for me to learn cooking, but in culinary art, I was a total failure.

The only thing I achieved was chicken congee which I made for my father's breakfast. Whether it was tasty or not (sometimes it was slightly burnt), as long as it was prepared by me, it met with his approval and he ate it all. Poor father, how much he must have loved me.

I also learned how to embroider slippers, something a girl of marriageable age at that time had to know besides cooking. It was customary that a bride include in her trousseau slippers for men and women, embroidered with her own hands, as presents for her in laws and relatives.

Thus, every day I struggled with gold and silver sequins and multi-coloured beads; disentangling knotted silk threads, pricking my fingers in a feverish endeavour to get perfect results, which of course I never did. I succeeded only in making myself feel frustrated. In all this activity, I had no time to think of anything else.

Then, one day, Fa-liong told me that Wan-hoei was in Medan and that he had invited him to dinner. I was surprised to hear this but thought nothing of it and was only a little curious. When Fa-liong came home that evening he called me aside and whispered: 'Wan-hoei asked me to give you this.'

He handed me something wrapped in a handkerchief. When I opened it, I found a letter and a photograph of Wan-hoei. Hastily, I read the letter written in English, a language which I could hardly understand. I remember only that he said he wanted me to marry him. At the bottom were a few Chinese characters which said 'matter important, decide quickly'. I could make little sense of it. He asked me to write to him in Penang.

I do not recall all that I wrote but it must have been silly and stupid. I remember only that I said if he truly wanted to marry me, he had to ask my parents for permission. A week later the reply came and was intercepted by my mother.

I was sleeping with my little sister (the newest addition to the family, just six months before). My mother pushed aside the mosquito net and said angrily: 'Look what you have done, shameless girl! How dare you write letters to men!'

Sleepily I rubbed my eyes and asked: 'What's it Ma?'

'What! Still pretending that you don't know what it's about? Here, read this.' She threw the letter at me. I got out of bed and went to the window to read it. I did not know why but my tears were rolling down my cheeks. Through the fog of frustration, I could decipher the word 'elope'. I did not finish the letter (I found out twenty years later that Wan-hoei had asked me to elope with him because he knew I was already engaged to someone else). Giving the letter back to my mother, I said: 'If this makes you so angry, I don't want to read it. Do with it as you like.'

My mother snatched the letter from my fingers and left the room. I went back to bed and cried my heart out. Why? I did not know; it was not for the wrong I had committed because I could not see the reason why it was wrong. I cried simply because I felt as if my favourite doll had been broken.

That afternoon, after my Chinese lesson, sister Song-jin came to my room.

'Aunt told me that you've been corresponding with a young man in Penang. You can't do this because you're engaged to someone in China.'

'What? Engaged!' I cried out. 'Mother never told me. Am I to be married and go to China?'

'Not so soon, of course. Come, let me show you something.'

She took me to our father's room and from the closet, drew out a photograph of a young man in traditional Chinese clothes wearing a close-fitting black hat. He had good features but his strange clothes did not appeal to me. Sister Song-jin unwrapped a red silk handkerchief containing a pair of gold bangles engraved with Chinese characters. Pointing to the photograph, she said: 'This is the man you're going to marry and these bangles are the tokens of your betrothal. Our uncle arranged this marriage three years ago when you were only thirteen.'

'Is it our father's wish that I marry this man?'

'Little sister, you know that once one's word is given, one can't take it back.'

'But it isn't our father's word.'

'Our father had to listen to his elder brother and besides, the family Lim had done a big favour for our uncle. We must therefore show gratitude.'

'Why not let cousin Fo-jin marry him'!' I asked.

'Fo-jin is older than their son, so they prefer you. Don't be sad, little sister,' sister Song-jin consoled me, 'you're going

Author with Tan Wan-hoei. She met him again twenty years later.

to be the daughter-in-law of a very wealthy and respectable man. This boy from Java had come with his father with the intention of calling on our father to ask for your hand in marriage. But when the father made inquiries, he was told that you were already promised to someone else, so, they left without seeing our father.'

Now I understood why Wan-hoei said in his first letter that the matter was important and that I had to decide quickly. Even if I had been romantic, I would not have understood the urgency at that time because I was totally ignorant of the state of affairs.

'Well,' I said, 'I don't care whom I marry as long as it will please my parents. I shall never write again to the boy in Penang or try to see him. I promise.'

Satisfied with my promise, sister Song-jin left the room.

In the meantime Wan-hoei's first letter and photograph which I had hidden among my clothes disappeared. Of course I knew that only my mother could have taken them away. I never asked her and no mention was made of him again.

One day, news arrived that the Manchu Government had been overthrown and that China had become a republic with Dr. Sun Yat-sen as the leader. All male Chinese cut off their pig-tails and the Manchu clothing was discarded for the modern Ming Guo fashion.

My late half-brother Kong-liang's widow, Kong-soh ('soh' means 'sister-in-law'), arrived from China with her four-year-old son. She related to us how the revolutionaries had wanted to kidnap the boy for ransom and how she dressed him like a girl for the escape out of the village in a sampan. They had had a hazardous trip before reaching their destination. Our house was now quite full.

My young life, hitherto so happy and uneventful, had become complicated by a broken romance, politics and intrigue. It was time for me to grow up.

Author's engagement photograph, aged 16.

Part Two

1

The matrimonial alliance

I HAD STOPPED going to school and was taking English conversation lessons from an Australian lady, Mrs. Smith. I don't know where my father found her, a nice elderly woman with a thin wrinkled face and greyish blonde hair. She was very patient and a good teacher. She made me pronounce *th* over and over again until I got it right. I practised it first of all on her name. At the same time, I continued with my piano lessons under a certain Mrs. Baay, a qualified piano teacher. It seemed to me that my parents wanted me to be the accomplished young lady I would have been had I been sent to a finishing school in Switzerland. But then the Lim family had requested an early marriage for their eldest son.

A distant relative of our late Aunt Liu had come with her two daughters to stay with us. Ahyat-yi was an excellent cook and helped in the kitchen. Her eldest daughter Soen-jin kept me company when I embroidered slippers for my trousseau. She was two years older than I and very good in needlework. As soon as my mother noticed this, she lost no time in choosing her to be my brother Po-liong's wife. Po-liong, the adopted son of Mother Lee, had arrived at the same time as Kong-soh.

The house in Poeloe Brayan needed repairs in preparation for the arrival of my future husband and his entourage. I heard this from sister Song-jin but hardly paid any attention to it. I felt as though none of these concerned me at all. It was strange that although my mother prepared everything for my marriage, she never said a word about it to me. Was she perhaps still angry with me over Wan-hoei? She merely scolded me whenever I made mistakes in my embroidery saying that I would make her

ashamed of having such an ignorant and incompetent daughter.
I thought how unfair it all was and why had I to learn all this
and for whom? No one had ever laughed at me and it was said
often enough, how nice and clever I was, having been to the
Dutch school with the Dutch children and now, suddenly, it
seemed I had become stupid! In any case, that was my mother's
incessant opinion.

Sister Song-jin told me that plans had been made for us
to go to Amoy, China, where the wedding was to take place.
But my mother objected to travelling with my baby sister who
was only a few months old. She suggested that the wedding
be postponed till the following year. The Lim family objected
to the postponement because everything had been arranged
for the date chosen by a fortune teller — the third day of the
tenth moon in the year of the Rat (1912). Besides, the political
situation in China at that time was somewhat uncertain. Dr.
Sun Yat-sen, whose wife I had met at the Pykett's less than
two years before, had become President of the Republic but
there were those who wanted monarchy without the Manchus.
Yuan Shi-kai, a former general under the Manchu regime, was

Standing from left to right: Author (age 16), half-sister Song-jin with
her baby, cousins Fo-jin (Aunt Liu's adopted daughter) and Fu-jin.
Sitting: Cousins San-jin and Yun-jin.

ambitious enough to create his own kingdom. Thus, after much consideration on both sides, it was decided that the wedding would be held in Medan.

***

Shortly before my marriage, sister Song-jin unexpectedly returned to China with her husband and children. Up to today, I cannot understand the reason for her sudden departure at a time when I so much needed someone who could enlighten me on the things I needed to know. My mother was so busy with the preparations for the wedding and caring for my baby sister that she found she had no time to spare for me. Thus the bride-to-be found herself all alone and feeling very neglected.

One of the big rooms upstairs was being prepared for the bridal chamber. I was not supposed to see it but at the request of the Resident's daughter, Minnie Rahder, who absolutely wanted to see the room before anybody else, I was allowed to accompany her. Minnie was a beautiful girl of 20, very tall with jet-black hair, magnolia skin and big dark eyes. When she smiled, an exquisite dimple showed in her right cheek. How I admired her beauty! Standing beside her, I appeared plump and very school-girlish. She looked at me and said pitifully: 'Imagine, Foek, you are going to be married in a few days' time! You look just like a little school girl. Don't you feel excited?'

'Not at all,' I replied with an indifferent smile, 'I just obey my parents.'

'Little goose,' Minnie commented and then turned away to hide her emotion.

Minnie admired all the things in the bridal chamber. The Chinese bed, the dresser, cabinet and washstand were of wood with delicate carvings and painted green, red and gold. The bed was decorated with a pink silk curtain, embroidered with phoenix and peonies. A variety of gold ornaments symbolic of joy and happiness hung in front of the curtain. Even the pink silk pillows were stitched with gold ornaments of very fine craftsmanship. On display in the glass cabinet was a complete gold tea set. In the dresser, piles of Chinese silk and satin of the most vivid colours lay open for inspection. On the washstand was a gold basin and water jug. Everything glittered and shone; it was a lovely sight. Minnie could not stop herself from exclaiming every time she discovered a new item more beautiful than the others and I joined in her excitement as if we were both envying someone else's dowry.

'How wonderful to own so much riches; to drink from gold tea cups and to wash one's face in a gold basin, not to mention the other things. You lucky girl! I wonder if a princess is given such a dowry.'

'Do you think this is all for me?' I asked innocently.

'Of course. This is your dowry. My mother told me that your mother had shown her the jewellery she is going to give you on your wedding day. They must be magnificent!'

'I don't know,' I mused, unimpressed by Minnie's revelation. 'I prefer the new doll Santa Claus sent me from Holland recently. It's a huge one with real hair and eyes which can close and open. It has a beautiful white lace dress, white socks and white leather shoes. She's about this high,' I said enthusiastically, raising my hand to my waist.

'Really!' Minnie said with a complaisant smile.

At that moment I could not grasp the importance and meaning of a dowry. It was only in later years that I learnt what effects a bride's dowry had. Some people had to sell or pawn their goods or go as far as to incur heavy debts simply to give their daughter a suitable dowry so that she would not be humiliated by the family she married into. That is why it was important that a matrimonial alliance should be well-matched in order to avoid disappointment and humiliation.

2
Wedding presents

FA-LIONG HAD GONE with Papa to meet my bridegroom who had arrived with his retinue in grand style. When he came home, he hastily greeted Mama who was feeding my baby sister and motioned me to a corner out of my mother's hearing and said excitedly: 'Do you know, Big Sister, that your husband-to-be is no taller than I! You must be at least a head taller than he.'

'I don't believe you, he is supposed to be twenty years old,' I retorted, almost with pride, knowing Fa-liong's usual playfulness.

'Well, you don't have to believe me but I tell you he is a dwarf. I have seen the little man and I even shook hands with him,' Fa-liong laughed mockingly.

I was not at all amused with this information. If what my brother had said was true, how could I wear my white satin shoes with high heels on my wedding day, I thought worriedly. For the first time in my life I was deeply concerned about my appearance and I decided that I must have the shoes altered. How ridiculous I would look if my bridegroom came only to my shoulders! I could not refuse to marry him, I could not disobey my parents who wanted me to be well married. I hoped that Fa-liong was only teasing but never theless decided that I must do something about the high heels. Without my mother's knowledge I cycled hurriedly to the shoe maker and asked him to cut away the heels.

'It will look very ugly,' the shoemaker protested.

'Never mind,' I said, 'and please let me have them back tomorrow otherwise I will surely get a scolding from my mother.'

Noticing my troubled face, the good man promised to do his best.

'I still have a piece of satin left from when I made these shoes for you. I shall make another pair with nice low heels, so don't worry.'

The guests had settled in our country house in Poeloe Brayan which for the moment was considered the bridegroom's home.

'You see, the Lim family doesn't want their son to marry into the bride's home, therefore they have to take a temporary house where the bridegroom can bring his bride, this is the custom,' Kong-soh explained when I asked her why we could not get married in our house.

'And besides.' my sister-in-law continued, 'the bridegroom's entourage is large: there is the maternal uncle, the matchmaker, Mr. Lam Lai-sang, two secretaries, one of whom is an English man, and his governess, an American lady. The governess even has a Chinese slave girl. Then there are four men servants and a cook — twelve people in all. I must not gossip, I have to see to the birds' nest soup; Papa has ordered me to prepare it and send it to the guests at Poeloe Brayan. Ahyat-yi and Po-soh (Soen-jin) have been cooking the whole day.' Kong-soh disappeared hurriedly into the kitchen when she heard my mother coming.

The next day, the pre-wedding ceremony when wedding presents were exchanged was held. My parents went to the Ancestral Hall to receive the delegates from the Lim family. Of course Fa-liong was with them, being the eldest son of the family. I had to stay in the back hall as if the ceremony did not concern me at all.

When the visitors arrived I heard animated whispers from the many relatives and guests.

'That's the maternal uncle in the lead with the matchmaker, the secretaries are behind them.'

'Little sister,' cried Kong-soh, 'go to your mother's room, you're not supposed to be seen, and certainly not allowed to watch!' She pulled me into my mother's room and told me not to leave it until the guests had gone. Ironically enough, I had no part whatsoever in everything that was going on. Friends and relatives were too preoccupied to bother about me, their curiosity was focussed only on the presents and the value of each item. Even my parents neglected me. I crept into bed and lay beside my baby sister who was sound asleep and wondered how it would be when she got married.

After a considerable time, Kong-soh came into the room followed by the maids who were assigned to me. They carried parcels in their arms. Putting them down on the table, Kong-soh said to me: 'Now you can have a good look at the presents.'

I jumped out of the bed waking my baby sister who started crying. My mother came in and took my little sister in her arms. 'She doesn't usually wake up at this time,' she grumbled, 'somebody must have frightened her.' I kept silent. After having fed the baby, my mother left the room telling me to look after my little sister.

I heard the motor car leaving and knew that my mother had gone out. I started to open the numerous satin boxes: red and white with gold decorations. The red boxes contained all the Chinese things: the traditional bridal suit, crown and jewellery — all of jade and pearls. In one of the white satin boxes there was a western bridal gown of white satin embroidered with pearls and a veil of very fine lace and orange blossoms. Besides these were other items, all foreign to me, as I had never seen real Chinese trinkets before. While I was looking through the gifts, Fa-liong called me: 'Big Sister, come and see what they have brought — candies and honey preserved fruits stacked five feet high.'

'Nonsense!' I answered, but nevertheless followed him to the ancestral hall. Indeed it was as he had said but as to what purpose those sweets served I had not the vaguest idea. I wondered how they could have been brought from so far and yet not get spoiled. That so much fuss was made over a wedding was beyond my imagination.

'And did you see the presents Papa gave to the bridegroom?' I asked curiously.

'Of course!' Fa-liong answered proudly, 'and I had the honour of handing the things to the chief delegate who received them with a solemn face and appreciative nods. There were trays with materials for suits, I don't know how many. Then neckties, socks and shoes, everything! There was also a box of jewellery…'

'Jewellery?' I interrupted, astonished.

'Yes, there was an enormous gold watch with a diamond chain, on which there was a big diamond star. There were also diamond cufflinks and a diamond tie pin. It must have cost Papa a fortune. I wish I were the bridegroom.'

'Don't talk nonsense! You'll have to wait till you get married and hope that your future father-in-law would be as generous and rich as our father,' I teased my little brother and made a face at him. How ironic it was. He was later to marry my husband's third sister.

From left to right: Fa-liong, Mother holding little sister Sze-yin, author, Kian-liong, Kwet-liong and Father.

3

Mother and father meet their future son-in-law

THE NEXT DAY, to my surprise, my father did not return to his office as usual after lunch. Instead, he spoke with my mother for a long time. They seemed to be discussing very important matters and we children were forbidden to eavesdrop.

At four, they started to dress, my father in his gold-braided white linen uniform and my mother in a very dressy gown of wine-red satin to which she pinned a corsage of orchids. As I took it for granted that they were going to attend some function, I did not pay much attention.

In the meantime, many lady relatives and friends had gathered in our house and were chatting very animatedly with Kong-soh who, being habitually placid, seemed to be in high spirits. I asked her curiously what was going on and why all these ladies were here.

'My little sister-in-law, don't you know that your bride-groom is coming to pay an official call on his father and mother-in-law? These aunts have come to have a look at the unknown bridegroom. But you, little sister, you are not to see the bridegroom, or he you, until the wedding day after tomorrow,' Kong-soh laughed amusedly. The ladies threw me curious looks and smiled mysteriously as if they were hiding a big secret. I was a bit irked. Why had my mother not told me about this visit? Had it not something to do with *me*?

My parents were in the reception hall to receive the visitors. All the ladies hurried to the screen separating the reception and ancestral halls. Pushing each other, they stood on tip-toe to peep through the open work of the screen, moving their heads constantly and whispering to one another. Those who did not have a good view suggested going to the small garden outside the reception hall. There, they could have a good look through the windows of the hall. Racing each other, they hastened to the garden and unconsciously, I followed in the melee.

I found myself behind the ladies regarding the strangers in the reception hall. I noticed that they wore foreign suits with neckties and among them was a foreign lady who seemed quite old. I heard the aunts say that she was the American governess. There was a young man sitting between my father and mother. Without a doubt he was the bridegroom. He was neatly donned in a light grey suit with a blue silk tie. His hair was parted on the left side. I compared his face with that of the youth in the photo sister Song-jin had shown me a year ago. That youth wore traditional Chinese clothes and a queue. Was this the same person, I wondered. To my relief, he was not as dwarf-like as my brother Fa-liong had described. Though I was not vain, I did not exactly relish the idea of a husband who was one head shorter than I. The day was sultry and hot. I felt stifled. I had seen enough and I went back into the house unnoticed. The excitedly chattering aunts never suspected that I had been in their midst.

When I was just passing through the ancestral hall, I saw my mother approaching, accompanied by the foreign lady. My heart sank. Had my mother seen me at the window? Her expression however was unusually mild.

'Foek, meet Mrs. Grey who wants to make your acquaintance.'

'Your daughter?' the lady asked amiably in English.

'*Ja*,' my mother answered in Dutch. She was clever enough to understand that 'daughter' and '*dochter*' sounded very much alike. The old lady extended a wrinkled hand on which she wore rings on each finger. I shook hands with her saying: 'How do you do?' in a very clear voice. Had Mrs. Smith, my English teacher, been there, she would surely have been very proud of me.

'You are sweet,' Mrs. Grey smiled showing a row of very neat false teeth. My mother guessing that her daughter was being praised pursed her lips as if to disagree but unable to find the words, acquiesced with a condescending smile.

Suddenly, I realised that the little Chinese girl who was standing behind Mrs. Grey was staring at me. She scrutinised me from head to foot. It was only after our marriage that my husband told me that Siauw-chui had reported to him after the visit and had said that my face was far from pretty, with big eyes, a flat nose and disfigured by freckles. My complexion was dark, she said, and I had big feet. Poor man, how he must have suffered thinking he was going to marry a horror of a wife! .

After the guests' departure, my mother came to the back hall where a few relatives still lingered. They wanted to hear what impression she had of her future son-in-law.

'My husband of course was very pleased,' my mother said. 'The young man is very polite and has good manners but he does not seem to be very robust,' showing clearly that she did not share my father's pleasure completely.

'They are very wealthy, this family,' said one of the aunts, 'your daughter is very lucky.'

'Well, these wealthy families in China also have funny customs,' my mother pondered, 'for instance, I understand from the uncle that the servant girls a bride takes with her to her husband's home will be eventually considered his concubines.'

'And what did you say to that?' asked the aunts who were ever ready for gossip.

'Of course I protested,' my mother answered with fervour.

'Custom in China or not, our custom here is one wife. My daughter was born in a country ruled by a Queen. Don't forget that! I was exasperated and if the uncle had not smiled good-naturedly at my outburst and apologised for his ignorance, I would have really broken the marriage there and then. Besides the Captain was looking at me imploringly. Just to play safe, I am not letting the two servant girls Kong-soh brought especially from the village accompany my daughter to her father-in-law's home.

4

'You are grown up now'

ON THE EVE of my wedding, Corry and Eddy Schoggers, my two best school friends whom my mother had chosen to be my bridesmaids, came to visit me. They were curious about the presents the bridegroom had brought from China. They admired all the beautiful things displayed in the red and white satin boxes. They, like myself, wondered whether the wedding gown would fit as I was not allowed to try it on. I told them to come early in the morning to help me dress and if it did not fit, we could still alter it. How naive I was! We chatted carelessly as if we were preparing for nothing but a big birthday party.

My mother was in Poeloe Brayan all day. I could not understand why she had to go there as the house was occupied by the bridegroom and his companions.

After dinner, Djamboel and Kwet (my third brother) were put to bed. Djamboel and his best friend Wim Kroese were to be page boys at my wedding. They were both six years old. (I only saw Wim again sixty-two years later when I visited Europe in 1974).

Old Nenek urged us to go to sleep but Fa-liong insisted on playing horses as we often did when my mother was not at home. I put a 'bridle' around Fa-liong's shoulder and taking a toy whip in my hand, I made him gallop. We ran in the gardens, through the back then to the front of the house like wild Indians, making all sorts of noises. Suddenly, Fa-liong tripped on the stone threshold of the front door. He squatted, holding his right big toe. It was bleeding. At the sight of blood, I cried frantically for old Nenek. She came running to us and grumbled: 'What did I tell you'! I'm sure you can't walk now.' Still muttering, she took Fa-liong on her back and carried him to his bedroom. Fa-liong's legs were almost touching the floor as Nenek was not much taller than he. I followed meekly behind. The old soul washed the toe and saw that the nail was broken. After putting *minyak kayu putih* (eucalyptus oil) on it she bandaged it with white gauze.

'Now, go to sleep. Both of you.' She lulled Fa-liong to sleep with one of her native lullabies though he was already twelve. I went to my own room and crept into the enormous double bed on which I occupied but a small corner...

I was woken up by old Nenek.

'Quick, get up.'

'What time is it'!' I asked sleepily.

'Four o'clock.'

'What for? It's too early, I want to sleep some more.'

'Get up! Don't you know that you are going to be married today'!' Nenek pulled me up. Rubbing my eyes, I asked:

'Is Mama up yet'!'

'Yes, come quickly unless you want to be scolded.'

I followed Nenek. In the meantime, Fa-liong in the next room, was already awake and complained that his toe was hurting him and he would not be able to wear shoes. Drowsily, I told him to cut a hole in his shoe.

'Come on now, I've prepared warm water for your bath. I will attend to your brother, don't worry.'

'A bath, so early in the morning'!'

'*Nonya Besar*'s (Big Mistress') orders.' We went downstairs to the bathroom.

After my bath, I heard a knock on the door and Kong-soh said: 'Here, little sister, your mother said that you must put these on.'

She shoved some garments through the half-open door and closed it again. I looked at the clothes — a white cotton jacket and trousers. I put them on reluctantly, finding them not pretty at all and wondered why I had to be dressed like this if I was to put on the wedding dress in the silver and white satin box.

Kong-soh was waiting outside the bathroom. On my appearance in the funny outfit, she smiled at me and said: 'You're grown up now.' I wondered what she meant but silently followed her to the ancestral hall.

My mother was already there talking to a woman whom I had never seen before. She was dressed in a *sarong* and long *kebaya* as a Penang nonya would. She was introduced as Madam Kooi.

Madam Kooi took me by the hand and led me to a big round sieve made of bamboo, in which was a low red stool. She told me to sit on the stool facing the ancestors' shrine. While my mother watched, she ran her fingers over my face. She seemed satisfied that there were no pimples and that the skin was smooth. Then she started to meddle with it. Taking a length of white sewing thread from a box, she held it between the thumb and second finger of her right hand, while with her left, she held the other end of the thread between forefinger and little finger. By twirling the thread, she pulled out the fine hair on my face. It hurt and I fidgeted on my seat. She told me to keep still, otherwise she might damage my skin. At this warning, I controlled myself as best as I could. After this operation, she plucked my eyebrows until she seemed it fit for a bride. My mother stood by, saying nothing and though tears came to my eyes because of the pain, her maternal love seemed only concerned about my appearance. Afterwards, my face was cleaned with a new towel soaked in soothing luke-warm water. Then my nails were attended to. Finally my hair which I usually wore in one or two plaits was done up high in the centre of the crown. Then Madam Kooi put white socks and gold embroidered red satin half boots on my feet. She dressed me in a traditional Chinese wedding costume which my mother had ordered from Penang. First she tied a green satin skirt embroidered with peonies over the pyjamas, then came an ample red satin jacket with very wide sleeves; over this she added a black sleeveless jacket which was equally elaborately embroidered. A crown with pearl tassles in front was put on my head and thus my matrimonial array was completed.

Author's bridal costume.

Madam Kooi led me from the sieve to the front of the ancestors' shrine. Then, my father and mother advanced to the offering table and seated themselves on the chairs which were placed on either side of it.

I had a glimpse of my father who looked very sad. Something gripped my heart, a feeling I had never known before. Then I heard Madam Kooi's voice saying: 'Kneel down,' at the same time pushing me into position.

'You are grown up now,' she continued, 'and you are going to leave your parents' home and enter that of your husband's. Thank your parents...' I heard nothing more, I broke down in uncontrollable sobs. With my head touching the floor, I wept as if my heart was breaking. My father bent over me and I heard him sobbing too while he tried to raise me to my feet with trembling hands. I clutched at his knees. He held me tight for a moment, as if he wanted to say something but no words came. Then, I heard my mother's stern voice.

'Enough, enough. Are you not ashamed? What are you crying for? Just like a woman!' she scolded my father.

My father turned away and hurried out of the ancestral hall.

5

The most beautiful bride of the year

HOLDING ME BY the arm, Madam Kooi led me to the back hall where many relatives were waiting to see the bride. Madam Kooi made me sit so that I could be admired. Praises went round. I was the most beautiful bride of the year, so they said. So young and innocent and yet so dignified, the equal to a princess. Stealing a glance at the grand mirror on the wall, I could hardly believe the fantastic reflection: a bride with a tear stained face. I wondered whether the admiration was sincere.

It was time for the wedding. I was relieved of the heavy traditional attire. Helped by my bridesmaids, the white wedding dress was taken out of its satin box and put on. It fit perfectly. On the front of the dress was sewn enormous diamond buttons. They were the Sultan's jewellery. He had insisted that I should wear them on my wedding day for good luck. They went well with my parure. Corry and Eddy cried out: 'You look magnificent!' No wonder. They could not recognise the playful friend they knew at school in this grandiose attire.

'Foek, you are worthy of your bridegroom, you will not shame him! As a matter of fact, any man would be proud of you.' I can still remember their enthusiasm, affectionate and loyal.

Looking at myself in the long mirror I saw a metamorphic change in my appearance. With my eyebrows plucked evenly and my hair done up on top of my head, I could hardly recognise myself. Poor ugly duckling! She could not believe she had become a swan. I sat down and let Corry and Eddy adjust my veil. Part of it fell over my face and the rest hung loosely over my wedding gown in a long train.

It was time. I heard my father's footsteps along the corridor leading to my room. He stopped in front of it, and asked: 'Ready?' Noticing my father's solemn face, I dared not answer, fearing I would cry again. I nodded and he gave me his arm. Obediently, I held it. My bridesmaids followed, holding my veil for all it was worth and in a stately manner, we went downstairs.

The house was packed with people. I could not distinguish them through my veil. Besides, I was told to keep my eyes cast down as befitted a bride. Everything seemed hazy. I had a bouquet of white orchids thrust into my hand and someone whom I assumed to be the bridegroom took my arm.

We walked in procession to the front door. I noticed Faliong limping painfully beside the bridegroom. The page-boys Wim Kroese and Djamboel skipped playfully behind me. Instead of holding the corners of my veil as instructed by the bridesmaids, they covered their heads with it, as would dragon dancers on New Year's day. The flower girls preceded us, strewing roses in our way.

The Sultan's black and yellow limousine, decorated with white stephanotis and silver ribbons, stood ready to take the bridal couple to Poeloe Brayan, the temporary home of the bridegroom where the ceremony was to take place.

At Poeloe Brayan we were immediately ushered into the bridal chamber where I recognised the nuptial bed which was in the bridal suite in our house. So, that was what my mother had been doing these last few days: she had improvised the matrimonial quarters such that I was to enter the bridegroom's house and not he into mine. Facing the bed was the long table on which now stood two gold and silver candle-sticks, holding two huge red burning candles decorated with dragons and phoenix.

Madam Kooi was already there and made me sit beside the bridegroom on the bed. In the meantime the bridegroom's uncle and Mr. Lam, the matchmaker, accompanied my parents into the room. Madam Kooi, as escort to the bride, told the bridegroom to lift the bride's veil. At that moment, I felt as if everything was swimming befre my eyes and I saw stars instead of people. We were led like two marionettes to stand before the long table which was arranged with various strange things.

First, the uncle produced two gold bands from small red velvet boxes and gave us one each to put on each oher's finger. They more or less fitted. Then Mr. Lam took the two satin scrolls lying on the table, handing one to my father and the other to the uncle. These were the marriage contracts which were already signed. We were married by the law of God.

When this was done, it was the job of Madam Kooi to give the finishing touch to the ceremony by giving us each a bowl filled with some edibles, and chopsticks. At the chanting of good wishes, she told us to feed each other. Suddenly I recalled brother Po-liong's marriage where at a similar ceremony the bride had refused to eat in spite of the bridegroom's solicitude. I almost forgot the solemnity of my own wedding and checked a laugh, which luckily evaporated, but could not help the twitching of my lips. We had to repeat this performance three times, each time with different food and Madam Kooi's propitious wishes.

The ceremony was conducted and we were mobbed by the wedding guests.

My father and mother left with the bridesmaids and the page boys. Fa-liong did his best to keep his dignity, enduring pain and trying to hide his limp. Thus I was left with my bridegroom and Madam Kooi who kept watch over us.

6

The unknown bridegroom

IN THE SUDDENLY quiet room, my bridegroom looked at me and silently invited me to sit down which I did gratefully, because I felt that I could not stand any longer. I sat heavily in the chair without too much grace, leaned back, and closed my eyes. Madani Kooi shook me by the shoulder and said softly: 'You can't go to sleep now. I'll get you some refreshment,' at which she left the room.

I felt as though I was in a nightmare. I looked around and met the gaze of the stranger before me. His eyes seemed to say, 'Are you alright?' I nodded. Our conversation without words was interrupted by Madam Kooi who entered with a tray of soup, two tasty looking dishes and rice. Again with his eyes, the bridegroom invited me to eat. This time we partook of the meal like ordinary people and not like marionettes.

Madam Kooi left us to our meal but, after some time, she came back, walking briskly to my side.

'I'll help you change into something more comfortable; this evening you have to put on your wedding dress again for the reception at the Big House.' As she was speaking in Hokkien, the bridegroom took the hint and left the room discreetly, letting down the embroidered silk curtains as he went. Madam Kooi took me behind a screen beside the bed and gave me a new pink silk dress to wear. When she had finished with me, she said that she was going to have a rest. I was not left alone for long, for the bridegroom returned and sat down beside me.

I stole a glance at my companion. He was not tall, it was true, but he had nice features with a tiny mole on his right cheek, thin lips and serious-looking eyes above a fairly high nose. He was agreeable and dignified and his manners were refined. As I was considering him, I wondered what he thought of me.

The silence was broken when two little boys burst into the room none other than Djamboel and Kwet, bare-footed and in striped monkey suits (one piece pyjamas). Djamboel announced: 'Papa says you can't go home until tomorrow, that's why we came to see what you're doing here.' He spoke in Malay and turning to the bridegroom, studied him with curious eyes. This must have embarrassed the latter because he asked me who the boys were.

I answered meekly: 'My brothers.'

Then he smiled at Djamboel and took him to the side table, pointing to the sweets on it. Djamboel did not wait for a second invitation and hurriedly filled his pocket with dried lychees, longans, sugared lotus seeds and would have taken more had I not stopped him. Turning round he saw Kwet looking longingly at the sweets so he filled his little brother's pocket as well.

'With whom did you come?' I asked.

'Just the two of us with the chauffeur. I wanted to know what you were doing among all the strangers. Well, we better go before Mama finds out.' And they dashed out of the room.

The Sultan's Fiat came to take us to the Big House. I wore the wedding dress but without the veil. Instead, Madam Kooi had arranged beautiful diamond flowers in my hair which made me look like a fairy princess. My bridegroom was in evening attire.

Corry and Eddy, my bridesmaids, were waiting in the front hall to escort us upstairs to the ballroom. I was dazed by the lights, the people and the flowers. There was warm applause when we appeared. Then there were handshakes, good wishes, hugs and kisses which I acknowledged rather dazedly. To stand there suddenly as a grown-up was beyond my comprehension. At that moment nothing seemed to register in my mind. I vaguely recognised Minpie, the Resident's daughter who a few days previously had admired my bridal chamber. She kissed me affectionately. My bridesmaids' parents hugged me with tears in their eyes. The Sultan and the Sultana who had seen me as a little urchin seemed prouder than my parents, if that was possible. Champagne flowed and toast followed upon toast.

When we returned to Poeloe Brayan that night, it was already eleven o'clock. Madam Kooi was in the nuptial room watching over the candles which must not be allowed to go out. My bridegroom motioned towards the garden and I followed him outside. Just as we were approaching the lotus-pond, two men suddenly sprang before us. They made themselves known as my father's most trusted bodyguards, Khap-ngee and Ah-hai and I recognised them in the dim lustre of the new moon. They used to take me by the hand when, as a little girl, I crossed the road from my father's office to our house. They spoke in Hokkien to my bridegroom, explaining that my father had strictly assigned them to watch the premises and that we were not to leave the house at all. They accompanied us back into the house like two naughty children. It could have developed into a romantic walk, perhaps, if not for that intervention.

Back in the house, we were separated to change out of our formal attire. Madam Kooi gave me the white cotton pyjamas which I wore in the morning. I thought it not seemly to appear before my bridegroom in them and I told the old lady so. But she replied that it was customary. I kept silent.

My bridegroom entered the room in a suit of white silk pyjamas. I could have cried with embarrassment. Madam Kooi made preparations to leave the room and told the bridegroom to mind the candles and not to let them be extinguished.

Without saying a word, I crept into the heavily ornamented bed with my face to the wall and fell into a deep sleep. I did not know when my groom came to bed but was suddenly awakened by the crackling noises that came from the candles. I turned and shook the man beside me frenziedly by the shoulder as if there was a fire. He got up and calmly cut the wicks with a pair of scissors, then came to bed again. This time, I became aware that I had been sleeping in the same bed with a strange man. Was this customary too? I wondered as I turned my face to the wall again. My bridegroom stopped me, murmuring some unintelligible words. I realised that something was about to happen to me ....

When I woke again, it was daylight. I found myself undisturbed in the crook of my husband's arm. Madam Kooi came to prepare me for our return to my parents' home and carefully folded up the white cotton pyjamas — a token of my virginity.

7

Prince Charming and his Princess

ON ENTERING THE bridal suite in the Big House, we were left to ourselves and having nothing to do, made an inspection of the spacious chamber. My husband (how strange this word sounded) made several unsuccessful attempts to engage me in conversation. I spoke Hakka mixed with Malay while his dialect was Hokkien. Thus, we could hardly communicate and if by chance he said something I could understand, I would mutter something to which he would always smile.

Thus ended our endeavour to become better acquainted that first morning. We sat in the straight-back, red-covered chairs of blackwood encrusted with mother-of-pearl, stealing glances at one another. Thinking of the events of the past day, I could not help but feel perplexed that we were still strangers and yet belonged to each other. How strange life was!

Prince Charming had found his beloved Princess and they had lived happily ever after. I wondered if they were strangers to each other in the beginning too? I smiled to myself and when I looked up from my musings, my husband was smiling at me. Was he thinking of the same thing or was he laughing silently at me?

At this moment, my sister-in-law, Kong-soh, came in followed by a servant girl carrying our lunch. Seeing our intimacy, she smiled broadly.

'My hearty congratulations, bride and bridegroom,' she said, 'as my new brother-in-law is still a stranger here, you'd better keep him company, little sister, don't think you can go downstairs to play with your brothers. You're no more a child but a married woman,' she finished teasingly. As she spoke our dialect, the bridegroom did not understand a word she said, or so I hoped. Fancy him seeing me play 'horses' with Fa-liong the night before our wedding! He might have refused to marry me.

After having laid the table, Kong-soh and the servant girl left the room. I tried to be a good hostess, and served the soup, but while handing it over to my 'guest', it spilled on the beautiful tablecloth. Seeing my clumsiness and perhaps fearing that I would upset the entire meal, my husband said in English: 'Never mind, I will do it myself.'

Author and husband Lim King-jin.

So, the roles were changed. Throughout the meal it was the bridegroom who served the bride. I was quite thrilled and for the first time in three days, I laughed. Being treated like a grand lady was beyond my expectations. Fancy sitting there happily enjoying my husband's attention. I had always been made to understand that it was the wife's job to serve her husband. I wished my mother could see me. She would have frozen me with her eyes.

The third day after the wedding, according to customs, was the day for the bride's parents, rich or poor, to give a banquet for their new son-in-law.

I was excluded from the feast as was the custom. As I sat brooding in the nuptial chamber, Djamboel's head suddenly popped out from behind the door, making mysterious signs with his hands. I did not understand what he meant and asked him to come in.

'Mama will not allow me to join the feast. She is afraid I would spoil or break something and bring bad luck,' he whispered.

I went to him. Dragging me by the hand, he took me to the balcony and pointed to the ancestral hall below. Indeed, we had a capital view of the feast. It was like watching a film in a cinema. Afraid of being seen, I hid behind the shutters while Djamboel lay flat on his stomach on the floor and watched through the rails.

'Look at *Ako Besar* (Big Brother),' he muttered in Malay, 'he has the air of a lord. Why is he allowed to join the grown-ups and I am not?'

'You are only a small boy, wait till you grow up,' I said.

'Such a pity I can't taste all that delicious food. I hope Kong-soh doesn't forget to keep something for me. Oh, look, they are making the bridegroom drink,' he called excitedly, 'I hope they don't make him drunk.'

I watched intensely as my husband took each drink which was offered to him. If he took just one sip from the silver wine cups, he was forced to empty the whole. So it went from table to table. The courses seemed endless. Old Nenek's voice gave me a start.

'So this is where you are. I've been looking for you all over the house. Munchung (Kwet's nickname because he has an elongated head) is already in bed. Come, it's ten o'clock,' she scolded Djamboel who put a finger to his lips.

'Sh! I'd better go before Mama catches me,' he said and disappeared with Nenek.

Left alone, I was no more interested in the noisy entertainment which became more and more animated. Feeling tired, I too went to bed.

I did not know what time my husband came in but was intensely aware of the heady smell of wine. My husband's face was very near me, I shook him off and almost pushed him out of bed. I was angry; I don't know why but I cried and swallowed my tears. A moment later, I heard him snoring.

The next morning, seeing my swollen eyes, he softly kissed them. He apologized for his inexcusable behaviour the night before and promised never to drink again.

'I shall never make these precious eyes cry again,' he whispered. And I shed more tears than an ocean could hold!

8

Apprehensions of a tyrant mother-in-law

WHEN MOST OF the excitement over the wedding had evaporated, we ventured out to the ballroom where we sat on comfortable sofas. It was most relaxing after the hard black-wood chairs in our bridal suite. We had just leaned back cosily, holding hands, when my mother's voice sounded shrilly from downstairs. My husband opened his eyes wide, enquiringly.

'My mother is scolding the kids,' I lied. My husband stuck out his tongue in awe. Actually, she was scolding us. As she spoke in Hakka, her new son-in-law could not understand although she meant him to. She was reprimanding us for having slept so late. Were we not ashamed to have lazed around while my father had already gone to his office? Hastily, I excused myself saying I had something to do. In fact, it was to meet the maternal wrath.

My mother having lectured me for what she considered rude also told me that I would be a failure in China. She then told me threateningly, that I would have to get up at fibe in the morning to prepare tea for my parents-in-law. She summed up all the duties I would have to perform as a daughter-in-law which did not include idling in bed with my husband. I could not withold my tears at hearing all the fearsome prospects lying in store for me. Of course, all my shortcomings, laziness, frivolities and ignorance were brought forth as usual. It served me right, she continued, if I were bullied by my mother-in-law in that strange and far-away country. It went on until she felt satisfied.

Coming upstairs again, my husband noticed my red eyes but he assumed that my tears were due to my fears of leaving home. Had he known the picture my mother had drawn for me of my future life, of being a servile wife and dominated by a tyrant mother-in-law — even he would have been horrified! However at that moment it seemed as though nothing but misery was awaiting me in that strange and far-away country. My mind was in complete confusion...

The next morning I told my husband that my father would like him to have breakfast with him. This was in reality my guise in order to avoid my mother's wrath. My father was very pleased that his son-in-law was so attentive and said that they would have all meals together in the future. So, we had won my father's heart forever, no matter what the circumstances were.

We had moved to my old room and my husband found my spacious spring bed far more comfortable than the oven-like nuptial piece which was rather impossible to sleep in with its ornaments and silk curtains.

In the meantime, Mrs. Grey, feeling lonely among all the menfolk in our country house, had come to stay with us. During our daily conversation, my English improved considerably, which however was not appreciated by my husband who wanted me to learn Hokkien because his mother only spoke that dialect.

As the time for us to depart approached, we were instructed by my parents to make our farewell calls. Only less than a month ago, I had dressed and behaved like a little girl and now, all of a sudden, I had to present myself in full length gowns with a hat to match. Though my appearance had the air of a grown-up, my manners remained as childish as always. Thus I was quite happy to have Mrs. Grey's company for our calls. The Dutch spoke English well and so the old lady was left to conduct the conversation to her heart's content while I just sat by, uttering a few words at appropriate times. I believe the governess had never felt more important in all her life.

The visit to the Sultan of Deli's palace was a great treat. Crowds of the Sultan's subjects were waiting in the brightly

The Sultan's Palace.

illuminated palace gardens to welcome us. As our yellow Fiat convertible drew up at the foot of the marble red-carpeted stairs, the guards of honour, wearing their uniforms of yellow and green, presented arms (lances).

Ceremoniously, we were brought to the Sultan who received us with affection.

'My daughter,' he said, 'welcome, welcome!'

The Sultana hugged me to her breast as if I was a little girl. Here, I was at home. Since I was a little girl I had often come here to play. Therefore, all their attention was paid to my husband and his honoured governess.

The lights of the chandeliers could not challenge the glitter of jewels worn by the Sultana and her ladies. Diamonds, rubies, emeralds and sapphires sparkled. The Sultan himself wore a black suit with silver embroidery, and on his jacket were the five enormous diamond buttons he had allowed me to wear on my wedding day. On his black velvet hat was a diamond the size of a pigeon's egg.

Veiled women peered through shutters and gazing around the screens whispered their approval of their guests of honour.

In the dining room, a banquet of sumptious Malay food was laid on a long table which shone with silver and crystal. The dishes contained no pork but mutton and beef were in abundance. All very spicy and hot. I whispered in broken Hokkien to my husband to avoid the chillies but not knowing the Hokkien word for it, I said it in Malay, which the Sultana understood, and she graciously offered the poor man a delicious plate of *sambal* (mashed chillies).

He never did forget his first taste of royal hospitality.

9

Queeny leaves her home

ALL TOO SOON the day arrived when I was to leave for my husband's home; my home too now, in Amoy.

It was a hectic day. All my numerous relatives and friends came to say goodbye. I was not to leave home alone because it was customary to equal the entourage of my husband. Accordingly I was to be accompanied by my mother's eldest brother, Uncle Kwee seng, her sister, Aunt Seh-han with her daughter, cousins San-jin (my Chinese teacher) and K'un-liong and as my special attendant, Otora, wife of our Japanese overseer in Poeloe Brayan. The reason for Otora coming along was that I would need her when we went to Formosa where everybody spoke Japanese. I was thus well equipped. The Sultan's private coach was attached to the engine. The Sultan, the Resident and other dignitaries were already in the coach when we arrived. As soon as we had boarded, the stationmaster blew his whistle and off we went. It was a special run. for us, to Belawan.

Aboard the ship, we were shown to our cabin which I found bigger than the one on the boat to Penang the year before. Was it just the year before? It seemed to me that unaccountable things had happened since. At the memory of that beautiful island surrounded by silver shores and emerald seas, a profound melancholy seized me. Was it a dream? Yes, a dream gone forever!

A gong gave the signal for visitors to leave the boat. I found myself in a rush of goodbyes and handshakes. Corry and Eddy kissed me tearfully. We promised to write each other. I saw my mother pass by without looking in my direction emotionless. I felt my hands gripped by my little brothers. Then everybody was on the quay. waving. but where is my father? I saw him coming fom the Captain's bridge, walking towards me. There were tears in his eyes. his lips quivered. but remained silent. My father turned to go, and I grabbed his sleeve. He tried to tear himself away but I clutched at his arm. crying frantically:

'No, no. I don't want to go. I want to go home.'

I don't know who separated us but through my tears I watched my father go down the gangway, not daring to look back. I moved to follow him but was held back by a sailor. I stood at the rails and sobbed my heart out. The next thing I remember was the ship's last whistle which found me lying in my cabin with Otora holding my hand.

***

My life away from home had started. Every mile was drawing me further away from the land where I was born and bred. I was no more the pampered daughter but a wife, a role I could not as yet grasp. I was entering a new existence entirely unknown to me.

At Singapore, we were entertained, one evening, by Mr. Wong Ah Fook. Papa's friend. There, I noticed a young woman. dressed in a formal black satin embroidered jacket and red skirt. She was a one-month-old bride (like me). She was Mrs. S.Q. Wong. the daughter-in-law of our host. We smiled at each other and in that one smile it seemed as if we had sealed a lifetime's friendship.

When we returned to the Raffles Hotel we found that Uncle Kwee-seng had met with an accident, in which he had seriously injured his foot. The next day, he had to return to Medan.

Next stop was Hong Kong. I had become terribly sea sick. Had it not been for the angel-like administrations of Otora, I would have been a complete wreck. It was cold when we disembarked. I was shivering and had no warm clothes. Mrs. Grey very kindly lent me a woollen shawl. I decided to go shopping for warm clothes.

Returning to the hotel, we were told by Mrs. Grey that our matchmaker, Mr. Lam Lai-sang had disappeared. He had borrowed a dress and hat from her and escaped through a window. I found the incident so comic and extraordinary that I burst out laughing. My husband joined in. But later, we heard his uncle say that it was no joke at all. Mr. Lam was a revolutionary and his life was at stake. I did not comprehend the implications at that time, but was to learn later that it was the period that Yuan Shi-kai turned against Sun Yat-sen and all revolutionaries had to flee for their lives .

After the stopover at Singapore and Hong Kong, we at last arrived in Amoy, my husband's home town, in the evening. The harbour was very pretty with the lights on shore shining brightly. We were all ready to go ashore. Leaning on the ship's railing, I saw a fleet of sampans approaching the steamer. A crowd of people came up the gangway. They went into the dining room and talked lengthily with my husband. Finally, they left with everybody except Otora, my husband and I. We had to stay on board until the next morning. I was not told the reason.

10

Here comes the 'barbarian bride'

WE WERE UP early the next morning. Otora had laid out my crimson, velvet dress with lace collar and cuffs. There was also a matching black velvet bonnet with two crimson roses. It was the only warm dress in my trousseau. My mother had instructed Otora that I should wear it when we arrived in Amoy.

A fleet of sampans with shouting boatmen drew alongside the steamer. I felt a little apprehensive to have to go into one of them. I looked at my husband enquiringly. He nodded his head and pointed to the shore. From the jetty, a big solidly built vessel was sailing towards us through two rows of small sampans on which were long strings of fireworks tied to bamboo poles.

My husband's uncle and another gentleman came on board and told my husband that we could now go ashore. As soon as we appeared on the gangway, firecrackers burst in ear-deafening noise; I covered my ears with both hands. This was the reception the sampan people wanted to give us and this was one of the reasons why we could not leave the boat the evening before.

We sat in the big sampan rowed by eight men in uniform: black Chinese suits with red trimming bearing the emblem of the Lim family. It was very impressive. Arriving at the jetty, a long passage of slippery stones, my husband walked ahead with his uncle. I followed hastily for fear of losing sight of him. Crowds of people lined the jetty but I had eyes only for my husband's back. I heard voices near me. They came from ladies who tried to catch my arms. There were four of them, two on each side and all were superbly dressed in formal black satin jackets and red skirts.

'Go slower, my bride, don't walk so fast,' they panted and held me in tow. I did not understand at that time what they said and what they wanted with me.

A sedan chair was brought forward and the ladies told me to get in. I stepped over its poles and hit my head against the canvas canopy. For a moment I stood still, feeling extremely awkward but was saved from embarrassment by one of the ladies who turned me round and helped me in. I was to go in backwards but I had never sat in a sedan chair before and knew no better.

It took only a few minutes before the chair was set down in front of a building. I was greatly relieved at the sight of my aunt and cousin San-jin sitting there, chatting with some people. Impulsively, I ran to them, sitting on an empty chair beside my aunt.

'We are staying here in this hotel,' my aunt whispered, 'you have to change into your wedding gown to meet your parents-in-law. So, you must listen carefully to what these ladies tell you to do.' The four ladies approached to take me upstairs.

'But I haven't had any breakfast and I'm very hungry,' I cried plaintively.

'Now, don't get upset, my little cousin,' cousin San-jin asserted, 'you can have breakfast later.'

After I had changed into my wedding gown, a large broad brimmed hat of white panama straw trimmed with small pink roses, was put on. The hat, half-concealing my face, was rather becoming and made me look the demure bride.

My escorts were always telling me to slow down. I wondered why, until I suddenly realised that they had tiny bound feet, shod in red embroidered shoes, not bigger than three or four inches. Downstairs, I looked longingly for the promised breakfast but no breakfast came my way.

In the hall, my husband was already waiting, dressed in a tailored coat and striped trousers, accompanied by two young men who wore Chinese formal long coats and short black jackets. My husband and I were helped into sedan chairs decorated with a red silk banner, carried by men wearing the same uniform as the boatmen. It was quite a procession, winding through lanes and streets where at every house and shop the firecrackers clapped their well-wishes. People were shouting: 'Here comes the bride!' and the more audacious one peered into my sedan chair.

We stopped at a Chinese style gate with two huge lanterns like the ones at home in Medan. Once more, thunderous fireworks greeted us. My inseparable escorts again appeared. They took me to a western style building and through a hall separating two spacious rooms. We entered the room on the left and I was struck by the mass of faces. The room was filled with people of all ages, beautifully dressed in silks of the most gorgeous colours.

My husband and I were led to the centre of the room before a long ebony table covered with an embroidered red cloth. On the right side was seated a gentleman wearing a dark blue brocade gown and black brocade short jacket. On the left, was a very handsome lady adorned in jade and pearl jewellery and wearing a gold embroidered jacket with an embroidered red skirt. They were my parents-in-law. I was given a tray with two covered tea cups on it. I was led to present the tea then led back to stand beside my husband. We were made to kow-tow three times. Then we met the rest of the family, invariably bowing to each. We were marionettes again as we were during our wedding in Medan. After this ceremony, my parents-in-law stood up. My father-in-law took the lead and my mother-in-law followed. My husband and I were right behind her. Noticing her tiny feet, I advanced to take her by the arm and helped her down the stone steps. I heard a roar of shocked voices from the ladies in the party.

'The bride ushering the mother-in-law, something new!' someone laughed.

As I did not understand what they meant, I continued to lead her by the arm indifferently and as we reached a wing of the house where there was a high staircase, I was glad to be of service again. It never occurred to me that a bride should abide by the instructions of her escorts. Thus my spontaneous behaviour was criticized as foreign and barbaric.

Our bridal suite was at the end of a corridor. We entered a sitting room and through a connecting door to the bedroom. I saw a double bed with brass fixtures over which hung a pink mosquito net and recognised my gold ornaments hanging from the canopy of the bed which was of red embroidered satin.

After having given some instructions, or so it seemed to me, my mother-in-law left with her retinue. Although she had not addressed me, her expression was kind and amiable.

A lady in a pale yellow silk jacket over a pleated pink skirt came over to me and said something which I could not grasp. I did not know who she was. When we were alone, my husband told me that the lady had said that I was to offer tea to visitors who came to see me. My faithful Otora, knowing my inaptness, was there to assist me.

'Who was the lady?' I asked my husband.

'Third Lady,' he said but that made me no wiser. I thought it was her name. Later I was to learn that she was one of my father-in-law's concubines. What a lot more there was for me to learn! It was a strange world, in which the only familiar person was my husband — still a stranger to me.

11

'Barbarian bride' becomes dutiful daughter-in-law

MY DUTIES AS a daughter-in-law had begun. My foreign ways clashed with many traditions and I was unanimously termed the 'Barbarian Bride'. Despite all these drawbacks and my language deficiency, I slowly became better acquainted with my husband's family.

My father-in-law was an extremely wealthy man. His wealth, coupled with his desires, acquired him six concubines who served his many needs. He tried very hard to make me feel welcome. For example, on the day after our arrival he gave us a conducted tour of his village and his properties. He even offered me his most treasured possessions — antique bowls and vases of the Ming Dynasty. But, for me, these were more of a burden than pleasure. I could not appreciate them. One day, my father-in-law chanced upon a cat walking on the mantlepiece on which the antiques were placed. The very next day they were removed. He could not bear to see his precious treasures so carelessly treated!

My tea-serving duty which lasted one month went by without mishap except for the morning when we overslept. Hastily dressed by the nervous Otora, we repaired to the drawing room where my father-in-law was sitting erect with a sullen face. We were half an hour late for which I was severely reprimanded.

During the month, we also took our meals together with the elders. I had to adhere strictly to their table etiquette; we were not to raise our chopsticks before the elders had done so; we were to wish them bon apetit before eating; we were to lay down our chopsticks when the elders had finished eating and say: 'Father-in law has eaten well' and 'Mother-in-law has eaten well'.

In this brief period, I also had the opportunity to get to know the various members of the family to whom I had been introduced on the day of my arrival. The first was my second brother-in-law, Ghee, one year younger than my husband, a handsome youth with pleasant manners. He was kind and tried to teach me proper Hokkien but unfortunately, I saw him only on weekends. Then there were brothers-in-law Lay, Tee, Sin, Keong and Quan (the latter two being boys of eleven and twelve).

My husband's first younger sister, Hong-koo, a small girl, was about my age. She had fine features but severe looking eyes and seldom laughed. She appeared very grown-up to me. Her hair reached to her ankles and she wore it invariably in one or two long plaits with a thin fringe which covered her forehead. She walked gracefully in spite of her bound feet and did not waddle like the others. I shied away from talking to her lest I showed my ignorance. On her part, she seemed uninterested in her new sister-in-law from a barbarian country. She seemed a favourite with my husband and they would spend hours talking and arguing over current issues. I, of course, could not understand what they were talking about in such rapid tones and confusing words or so it seemed to poor me. Most of the time, I was left out of their conversations and just sat there like a dummy. On top of it, they would roar with laughter when I said something unintelligible in my Penang Hokkien.

Father-in-law had his meals in his private apartments served by his concubines, Third Lady and Fourth Lady. The latter also served Mother-in-law, once in a while when she did her hair. The process sometimes lasted half a day. Instead of washing the hair, which they thought would bring on a cold, it was combed for hours with a fine-toothed comb until all dirt was removed. The hair was then oiled and smoothened thoroughly, so that it looked like lacquer. The long strands were then coiled into the shape of a butterfly or a cicada and decorated with jade and pearl hairpins. Sometimes a bouquet

Mother-in-law.

of jasmine was added for their fragrance. I was fascinated by Fourth Lady's apt and nimble fingers which could manage such a complicated task as if it was child's play.

While my mother-in-law played cards I stood behind her watching. Although I did not understand the game, it was my duty to stand by lest she wanted something. I was to call a servant girl, for instance, should she want some tea or wanted to light her silver water-pipe. I have never seen Mother-in-law smoking a cigarette. She kept to the old-fashioned water-pipe which only the high ranking ladies of that time smoked.

My mother-in-law, contrary to the grim picture my mother painted of her, must surely be one of the sweetest and most dignified persons I've ever met. Whereas everyone else treated me as a foreigner in those early days, she encouraged me and boosted my morale in a world that was strange to me. Once my mother-in law's eldest sister, a very frank woman, came from the village. She was full of criticism.

'Your daughter-in-law is far from beautiful,' she said to my mother-in-law, 'her features are too outlandish and what horrible big feet she has. Is she by chance a "barbarian princess"?'

Her conception of a beauty was someone as slim as a willow, flat-00chested, with narrow hips and feet 3 inches long. She was to have a face shaped like a melon seed, eyebrows curved, eyes like the autumn flow, a mouth like a cherry and nose too delicate to breathe. I had none of these qualities.

My mother-in-law smiled. 'No matter how she looks or who she is, she is just the wife I had wished for my son.' Yes, indeed, my mother in-law was far from the fire-breathing tyrant my mother said she would be. Instead she was gentle, tolerant and cultured. In every sense a grand lady.

I was becoming more and more familiar with the household and the numerous relatives. There was one dark-skinned middle-aged woman who was called Mui-ah. Although she had the appearance of a servant, her familiarity was unrestrained with my parents-in law. I was told she was a servant girl of my husband's late grandmother and was playmate to my father-in-law when he was a small boy. Thus she enjoyed a certain privilege in the family.

I would have liked to present myself as a Chinese rather than a foreigner to my father-in-law's family whom I was to visit, but I had no Chinese clothes in my trousseau. So, wearing a flowing brocade dress of apple green and matching picture hat with a pink ostrich feather curling on one side, I presented myself to Mother-in-law for her approval.

'You look very pretty,' she said. 'Don't pay any attention to what people say; those in Amoy are extremely conservative.'

Father-in-law and some of his children.

We set out — Father-in-law, my husband and I with Mui-ah as our escort. When our sampan got to the other shore, our sedan chairs which had been sent ahead were already waiting. We were set down in front of a mansion. People were there to welcome us, eyeing me with intense curiosity, darting glances at each other. I felt like an animal in a zoo. This thought threw me into bewilderment but luckily, remembering what Mother-in-law had said to me, I remained calm.

We were ushered up a dark and narrow staircase. On top of the stairs, a middle-aged lady in a red skirt and grey silk jacket welcomed us profusely, calling Father-in-law 'brother'. I was introduced to a number of uncles and aunts, all in festive attire. But the person I remembered best was Hua-ko in whom I found a great likeness to Father-in-law. My husband explained that Hua-ko was Father-in-law's real sister. Father-in-law was born into the House of Tan, but was adopted when he was very young by his aunt, who had married into the House of Lim, as she had lost her son in infancy. Thus, he became the legal son of the House of Lim, which many years later was to have three more sons borne by the second, eighth and ninth wives.

My recollections of my father-in-law's immediate family are vague. I never went back again to the House of Tan.

***

I was to meet more members of the family. I had to serve tea to two old ladies who had arrived from Taiwan, Sixth and Eighth Grandmothers. They were a pair of kind, simple and unassuming elders whom one could not help but respect and love. They eyed me with approbation and congratulated my mother-in-law for having chosen such an appropriate daughter-in-law. Opposite them stood a row of boys and girls. I met Fourth Uncle Peck (Eighth Grandmother's son), a jovial youth of eighteen with distinguished features and a rosy skin. He grinned when I offered him tea according to custom as he was of a higher rank.

Uncle Peck did not affect the air of an uncle. On the contrary, he was equable and was constantly in our company rather than in that of the adults. Our sitting room became the gathering place with my husband as the leader. Everybody called him *Toa-ko* (Big Brother). Unlike my first sister-in-law, the new arrivals showed interest in me. They asked all sorts of questions about the land where I came from and did not treat me like a barbarian. They did not laugh at my childish speech. I felt happy and at home. I joined the younger sisters-in-law when they played hide-and-seek in the back garden, watched by an amused Sixth Grandmother. We were cautioned by Third Lady for laughing too loudly but that did not deter us. I had never felt so happy and free since I set foot in China.

One afternoon, we went for a long walk to the plot of land in which my father-in-law cultivated chrysanthemums as a hobby. The land was flanked by the sea, with its silvery shore, and a cliff with shady trees on top. To the right was *Ho-tau-shua* (Tiger-head Hill). It was a lovely spot. Father-in-law later turned the chrysanthemum plot into a garden with picturesque Chinese cottages and pavilions. He added a balustraded granite bridge along the bottom of the cliff across the rocks on the shoreline where we watched the rhythmic waves play with the sand. At the end of this bridge was a stone terrace where we could enjoy the sunset. Running along the cliff was an artificial grotto winding upwards to the top where a small stone house stood among a grove of cassia, peach and plum trees. It was a heavenly retreat.

'Here, I want to rest forever,' Mother-in-law had said once when Father-in-law asked how she liked it. So, when the gentle lady was laid to rest, her coffin was conserved for more than two decades in that stone house before it was put to earth on the very spot. As memories of those enchanting days come back to me, I realise that my mother-in-law's undying soul is the eternal possessor of that garden in spite of all the world's changes.

12

King and Queeny

IT WAS MY first New Year's Day away from home. I was the only one in European dress and notwithstanding my brilliant appearance, I felt a little out of place. But dear old Mrs. Grey was there to compliment me and she said I looked like a queen. From that day, I was Queeny, which was most appropriate because my husband's name was King-jin and everyone called him King.

We went to Taiwan to visit the Lim family's Ancestral House where my husband was born. Taiwan was, at that time, Japanese territory. Therefore my husband was a Japanese citizen and we had to have our marriage registered under Japanese law.

I stepped upon Taiwanese soil a very weak and sick woman. The Formosan Straits was reputedly one of the worst stretches of sea, and I was terribly seasick. However, I recovered my spirits after a good meal and a rest. We set out for the Ancestral Home.

A high wall surrounded the extensive compound and two gigantic granite lions stood at the entrance of the mansion. We entered the front hall with enormous painted wooden pillars and gilded carved doors which opened to a granite courtyard. Across it was the ancestral shrine, its fittings stained with soot, a sign that generations had worshipped there. Everywhere, there were gilded characters and encrusted decorations. The forefathers were high-ranking Mandarins and had expanded the mansion as the family grew. In the last century, an annex garden was built. It was a replica of the *Ta Kuan Yuen*, the garden named in the Chinese classic *The Dream of the Red Chamber*. We visited the garden. It was delightful.

There were picturesque houses, chambers, and red humped bridges leading to tea pavilions where one could take refreshments while admiring the goldfish in the pond. It was the beginning of summer and the nemophilia and water lilies were at their best. Red, pink, white and yellow blooms filled the garden with a rush of colours. There was also a nunnery with a pagoda which cast a serene effect on this fantasy land.

We had lunch in a pavilion in the centre of the lake where carps played. Tea was served by two servant girls clad in colourful silk tunics and trousers. It was fascinating and romantic!

'Before the Japanese took over, my father was lord over this place and he did not fail in the role of Chia Pau Yue,' my husband laughed and Uncle Peck asserted, 'We were born too late, my nephew.' Both smiled enigmatically.

I was intrigued.

'And who was Chia Pau Yue and why should Father-in-law impersonate him?' I asked innocently.

'Wait till you have read the book,' my husband promised.

When we got back to Taipei, my husband presented me with the book. I could read enough Chinese to find myself immediately absorbed in the romance of *The Dream of the Red Chamber*.

Soon after my visit to Taiwan I became pregnant. Ironically, I was the last to know of it. Everyone else had recognized the symptoms. It was my mother-in-law who told me.

'Take good care, don't run about too much. My son told me that you are pregnant.'

I was bewildered.

Father-in-law came over from the Big House, glanced at me and went to Mother-in-law to learn the exact position of my case. He was going to celebrate his fortieth birthday the next year and was proud and enormously satisfied that, by then, he would already be a grandfather.

Another event that was to cause a lot of excitement that year was Uncle Peck's wedding which was celebrated with great pomp. No expense was spared. Everything was made worthy of the son of the late mandarin Lim Si-hua. A horse carriage was ordered from Shanghai to replace sedan chairs for taking the bride and bridegroom in procession through the small island of Kulang. A Peking opera had been engaged for a month to entertain guests during dinner. There was no end to the festivities. Men were carried home drunk, only to reappear the following day to continue their 'finger game' to decide who was the best drinker.

Thus, my first year in China flew past very quickly in luxurious surroundings. I was learning to be more and more at ease in my husband's home which had also become mine. In all those youthful and carefree days I had not known any kind of unpleasantness. All too soon another year had passed bringing with it my first taste of misery.

13

My first taste of misery

IT WAS MY second New Year's Day away from my parents. On that day when everyone was celebrating, I saw among the well-wishers a young woman whom I had never seen before. The servant girls and maids threw glances at me as if to convey some meaning which they did not dare speak. After having seen Mother-in-law, the young woman passed me with a strange look of censure in her sensual eyes. Her wide mouth was parted in a smile of faint mockery; she was rather pretty and her manners were beguiling. She seemed to be quite at home. Confidently, she went through the corridors and entered the room where my husband was playing Mahjong with his sister, Kooi-chee and Fifth Aunt, Mother-in-law's younger sister. I saw her standing behind my husband's chair with her hands resting lightly on his shoulders. He did not look up, apparently too absorbed in the game. I was annoyed by her familiarity. She could not be a relative or she would have been introduced to me. However, pretending not to be interested, I turned away. Mui-ah was walking past me. I stopped her and asked: 'Mui-ah, who is that young woman in the blue silk suit?'

'Oh! That one!' answered Mui-ah with disdain, 'she used to be Supreme Lady's servant girl. She and First Young Gentleman had an affair.'

'What affair?' I asked ignorantly.

'Well, she seduced him in anticipation of becoming his concubine when he marries. But your mother-in-law came to know about it and immediately packed her off to her mother in the village. That was three years ago and she has never been back since. She had heard about the Peking opera and was curious to see it. I heard Supreme Lady tell her never to come again.' Mui-ah had said all this in one breath and finished with a sneer in her 'matter of fact' tone: 'Shameless woman!'

I was bewildered and did not know what to do. I had to control myself and not give way to my unhappiness. It was as if something had broken inside me, a pain never experienced until today and I had nobody to turn to, to confide in. Mui-ah must have told the truth because she was a simple soul who considered the intrigue and craftiness of the servant girls as something natural. Their only ambition was to gain favour from their masters.

That night, we walked home in silence, interrupted occasionally by some remarks from my husband which I did not hear. In the dark, he could not see the tears trickling down my cheeks. As soon as we reached our room, he looked at me and asked impatiently: 'What's wrong? Has someone insulted you?' as if he already knew the reason for my distress.

At this provocation, I could not bear it any longer and answered bitterly: 'Yes, I have been mortally insulted,' letting loose a torrent of tears and halting words mingled with heart-broken sobs.

He did not deny his past folly but refused to admit he had given the woman any illusion of becoming his concubine.

'Why do you worry? All is past,' he said indifferently, 'she is married now.'

I was sitting on the bed and my husband came to sit beside me.

'Don't cry any more, your eyes will be swollen. Come My Heart ...'

Pushing him away, I cried: 'Don't! Don't ever call me by that name again. You must have called her that too. I accepted you as my husband and respect you as an elder brother who will love and protect me. Now you have killed all the faith in me.' I buried my face in the pillow.

Hearing the row, Otora appeared in the door.

'Don't harm yourself, my lady. It's bad for you. Let me wash away your tears and have a good sleep. Tomorrow, everything will be alright again. Married couples do quarrel sometimes but it's like flowing water washing away the impurities.'

Early the next morning, my husband woke up but I wanted to sleep on, too lazy to go with him to Mother-in-law's. He went alone. We had not made any attempt to make up.

Two hours later, Ming-hsian, the young valet came upstairs.

'The Young Master has taken ill at Supreme Lady's place. Second Young Gentleman brought him home and they are now downstairs in the drawing room.'

I dressed hastily wondering what had happened. Entering the drawing room, I saw my husband lying on the sofa and brother-in-law Ghee sitting by his side.

'Big Brother had a slight heart attack. Dr. Hartley has examined him and said it was not very serious but he needs complete rest,' Ghee explained, reassuring me.

I approached my husband and took his hand. Tears fell on it. They were my tears — tears of remorse. I feared that I had driven him to despair.

***

For the next two weeks, second brother-in-law Ghee and I were the only ones who were constantly with the patient who lay flat on his back, spoke in murmurs and showed his wishes only by signs. He seemed very weak. At night, Ghee and I took turns in vigil, sleeping in the armchairs of the drawing room. One morning, I woke up to see my brother-in-law staring at me.

He grinned and led me to the big looking glass with the gilded frame.

My face was swollen from mosquito bites. It looked pathetic and like a clown's face with red spots painted on his white mask. It drew a worried smile from my husband. That evening I was given a camp bed with a mosquito net fixed on four bamboo poles.

Three weeks passed without complications and after a consultation with our house physician, Tai-pit, Dr. Hartley declared that his patient was on the way to recovery. He was allowed to sit up for a couple of hours a day. What he needed now was diversion but no excitement whatsoever. The nightly vigil was no longer necessary but we left Ming-hsian, the valet, in my place on the camp bed, in case of an emergency. However, the recovery was uneventful and we concentrated on finding ways to distract my husband's attention from his illness.

My father-in-law had arranged a double wedding for his sons Ghee and Lay. I had to admire my father-in-law for his versatility in doing things in grand style; first there was Uncle Peck's splendid wedding and now the twin wedding for his sons. These were occasions to be remembered for a long time, for grandmothers to relate to their children and grandchildren.

In all these activities, it seemed that my first quarrel with my husband was forgotten. But deep in my heart, I still felt the pain; a wound which would leave a scar in my life. Had I been more mature or had I learned more about human nature, I would have perhaps understood and accepted its cause. However, the blow fell on unprepared ground, destroying trust and faith in the fray of emotionalism. My only thought was naive: how would he have felt, had I not been a virgin?

Standing from left to right: Brother-in-law Ghee's wife, author,
brothers-in-law Quan and Ghee, and author's husband King.
Sitting: Father-in-law with Fourth Lady, Fifth Lady and little sister-in-law.

14

Queeny's little prince

MY PREGNANCY did not bother me in the least, so much so that I did not realise that my time for delivery was due. My mother-in-law saw to it that I had all that I desired at this time. She looked after me with great patience and gentleness. One night I felt an uneasiness assailing me which prompted Otora to inform my mother-in-law. That night, I brought a boy into the world.

When the baby was shown to me the following morning, I noticed a blue mark on its right ankle. Wondering whether it was a birth mark, I asked the midwife.

'Oh, that,' passing her finger lightly over the spot, 'this naughty boy wanted to play a trick on us by showing only one foot, but got nipped, then changed his mind and entered the world properly on both feet. He gave me a fright!' She shivered at the thought of it. She made me laugh thinking that she had made a joke of the fact which, I was to learn much later, had been a real miracle.

According to my mother's instruction, I was to nurse the baby myself. As he was put in my arms, I was completely ignorant of how to go about it and Otora had to help me. Feeling the nipple against his tiny mouth, it began to suck but not a drop of milk appeared. It made several attempts without success. Just at that moment, Dr. Hartley came for his round and was astonished to find my nipples tightly closed, with no sign whatsoever of a pore from which the milk could flow. He ordered the midwife to massage my breasts and when this failed to make them function, he prescribed perforated rubber plasters to be applied on both breasts. He left with conviction that that would be successful. When this did not help, my mother-in-law lost faith in barbarian methods and consulted a Chinese *sinseh* (herbalist doctor) who arrived with a paste of finely ground herb which was to be smeared all over my breasts. This did not help either. Four days passed and my baby was being fed only on sugar water. Then an old lady told Mother-in-law to find a bigger baby to suck out the obstinate milk. A baby boy of about one year old was laid at my breast. He had not been fed for more than three hours and was hungry. When he felt my nipple he opened his mouth and nipped at it hungrily. I shrieked with pain and pushed the poor child away with all my might. I lay back exhausted. Mother-in-law refused to listen to any more advice. She did not want her first grandson to starve. As if she had foreseen all this, she had a few days earlier engaged a wet-nurse, a fat, healthy young woman from the village with breasts like pumpkins.

As for myself, the worst was yet to come. The pain in my breasts subsided but left me in a listless state. According to old fashioned ideas, I was supposed to be up and about only one month after delivery. At Mother-in-law's daily inquiries about my condition and appetite, I just answered that I was eating well. I lay there looking out of the window at the budding blooms of spring and at night I gazed unseeingly at the starlit sky until sleep overcame me.

One morning, however, Otora, preparing to wash me felt that my body was burning with fever. Dr. Tai-pit was immediately sent for (Mother-in-law had totally lost confidence in the English doctor). My fever was 104°F and on retrieving the thermometer from under my arm, Tai-pit discovered a swelling on the side of my left breast — a boil ready to burst. He became very agitated and began to stutter incoherently. Mother-in-law lost her patience.

Without much ado, the doctor told me to turn my face away. I heard him ransacking his medicine case and before I knew what happened, I felt a gush from my breast. After a long while, he heaved a deep sigh of relief. He showed me a spittoon full of yellowish fluid that had been my milk. Mother-in-law was horrified at what had narrowly escaped her grandson.

'If... y... y... you... had not s... s... s... s... sent for me today ... to... tomorrow... would have b... b... been too ... la... la... late, he said, still stuttering. He explained to my husband later that the poison would have spread to my heart. Whether it had been an exaggeration or a fact, I am and will be forever grateful to Dr. Tai-pit for having saved my life. Thus ended my attempts at breast feeding, leaving my breasts more or less like deflated balloons. And my baby soon became the sole property of my mother-in-law who doted on him to the exclusion of everyone else.

15

The celebration

FATHER-IN-LAW's fortieth birthday came.

The right wing of the Big House below my parents-in-law's apartments was transformed into the ceremonial Birthday Hall. In the centre of the wall hung a large scroll of red satin embroidered with a huge character for longevity in gold threads. Below it on a long ebony table stood gilded candle-stands in which burned two big red candles decorated with dragons and phoenix. Placed in front of this was a square table on which were displayed symbols of birthday celebrations: long life noodles, red dyed buns made in the form of peaches, honey preserved dates, prunes, mandarins and lotus seeds. On both sides of it stood porcelain pots in which mandarin orange trees grew. These were also tokens of luck. Along the other three walls were arranged red scrolls embroidered with the gods of Longevity, Happiness and Prosperity and lengthy handwritten birthday congratulations in poems or verse presented by friends and relatives. From the awning hung red banners and silk lanterns which led in long procession to the front gate. A Chinese string orchestra played melodious music enhancing the atmosphere of celebration and visitors were ushered in with beats of a brass gong. Attendants stood by the desks with brush and ink as guests signed the guest book.

At the appointed time, the Master of Rites announced in a sonorous voice that the ceremony for the household was going to start. We trooped in orderly parade, the men from the right and the ladies from the left and stood in rows on both sides of the Hall. It was indeed very impressive, the sons in uniform attire, dark blue gauze (summer wear) long coats with the short black gauze *Ma-kua* (jacket) and the married young ladies in black tunics and red skirts. For this occasion, I had Chinese clothes made for me. The four sisters-in-law wore long pink coats and short jackets like the men's but in different colours. The three concubines wore pink pleated skirts topped with canary yellow tunics. Mother-in-law's tunic was the most outstanding. It was embroidered with jade and pearl flowers. Rank and position were distinctly observed.

As soon as the parents had taken their seat at each side of the square table, our names were called. My husband and I were the first pair to pay our homage, followed by Ghee and his wife and then Lay and his. Then came the four unmarried sons, Tee, Sin, Keong and Quan. The four daughters followed suit. My son, Tong, only three months old, dressed in a long red coat and black jacket in the arms of his wet-nurse, paid his respects to his grandparents. A murmur of approval went round the room at his appearance; everybody had been waiting to have a look at the first grandson. My parents-in-law beamed and when the wet-nurse had stood up after kneeling down, Father-in-law motioned her to come nearer. He caressed the boy on the cheeks and Mother-in-law did likewise. Afterwards,

Father-in-law on his fortieth birthday, 1914. Standing from left to right:
Four unmarried daughters, three daughters-in-law, three concubines,
three married sons and four unmarried sons. Sitting: Mother-in-law
and Father-in-law with baby Tong on his lap.

the three Ladies advanced together to render their reverences. When Sixth and Eighth Grandmothers appeared, my parents-in-law stood up, embarrassed, to receive their good wishes while Uncle and Aunt Peck paid homage as younger brother and sister-in-law. After this, Mother-in-law's brothers and their numerous families paid their respects.

Then my parents-in-law retired upstairs with the grandmothers and the rest of the household, leaving only the sons to attend to the well-wishers who arrived in crowds. It was polite and traditional that visitors make felicitations at the Birthday Altar while it was proper on the part of the jubilarian to be absent. Instead, the sons bowed in thanks. No words were exchanged, they came and went with the understanding that they would be back in the evening for the feast.

The whole courtyard was illuminated with coloured electric lights and the banquet was splendid and gay. There were lots of drinking, toasting and the unavoidable 'finger-game'. The wine was served by 'sing-song girls'. It was the first time that I had seen these girls who were usually in attendance only at 'stag parties'. The celebration lasted till the small hours of the morning when many, having had a drink too many, had to be carried to their sedan chairs.

Part Three

1

Queeny meets a realist —
Mr. Lee Kong Chian

IN THE OLD days, a married daughter did not visit her parent's home after her marriage (no matter how near the families lived from each other) until invited by her parents. For, if the daughter arrived unannounced, her parents would suspect that she must have offended her parents-in-law and had been sent home. Thus, it was not until the birth of my son Tong, did my father write to my father-in-law inviting my husband, the baby and I to visit them. After a long discussion, permission was granted for me and my husband to go, but we had to leave the baby behind.

Though fully recovered from his illness, my husband's constitution was delicate. He adopted the habit of walking with a stick like an old man (he was only 22). He refrained from excitement. The only pleasure he found was in his books. Our married life had temporarily become a companionship without conjugal duties. I treated him like a big brother and from then on called him so (I had never called him by his name nor had a pet name for him). I never mentioned our first quarrel again and wished to be a friend rather than a possessive wife.

In the wake of 1914, we started our journey home via a roundabout route. First, we visited Japan where we spent a glorious month with brothers Tee and Sin, who were studying in Tokyo. Then, we went to Kyoto, the ancient feudal capital, where the Imperial Shrine is. We left Japan in a luxurious N.S.K. liner, the *Suwa Maru*.

We occupied a special suite, laid out with every comfort and luxury which could be provided at sea. The steward and stewardess assigned to the cabin were well-trained and seemed impressed by our valet, Ming-hsian, who was indispensible to Big Brother.

The purser inquired whether we preferred to have our meals in the Dining Saloon or to have it served in our suite. Before Big Brother could answer, I said we would prefer to eat in the dining room. I wanted to see everything on this floating palace.

We were ushered to the Captain's table where the Master welcomed us in Japanese. We were seated on either side of him and were introduced to two elderly couples from New York and a rather arrogant Englishman who wore a monocle.

In the course of conversation, one of the ladies asked me whether we were on our honeymoon. I told her that we had already been married for two years and had a son of five months. These foreigners were curious to know what precedence we had over them, the so-called 'superior race'. They were all insolent and haughty, much to the disgust of Big Brother. After this unpleasant encounter with these Westerners, we kept to ourselves.

We had been the only Chinese on board, but after stopping at Shanghai, we were glad to note that many of our compatriots had joined the cruise. They were in the second class, but this did not prevent Big Brother from making their acquaintance. However, they were all Cantonese businessmen with whom he could not make himself understood. Luckily, there was among them a young man who spoke the Amoy dialect. Big Brother introduced himself and found that they were from the same province. His name was Lee Giok-kun alias Lee Kong Chian. He had studied in Shanghai and was now returning home to Singapore. Big Brother invited him to our suite and from then, Mr. Lee became a regular visitor.

The two new friends would talk for hours and stopped only at the sound of the 'gong' calling them for meals. Big Brother's sulkiness gradually disappeared and everyday he sought new topics for discussion. Sometimes, I could not follow their conversation and Mr. Lee would then explain everything patiently to me; he did not ridicule my ignorance which was usually the case at home in Amoy. Mr. Lee seemed to understand that I was born in the Southern Seas where women were taught only domestic affairs. Slowly, I became more interested in things beyond my small world. I realised that one way of learning was to listen. I seemed to have really grown up.

The days passed and the friendship deepened. Waving aside all formalities, Mr. Lee now addressed my husband who was several months older than him as Big Brother and me, Big Sister-in-law. As much as Big Brother was an idealist, Mr. Lee was a realist. He told Big Brother that by avoiding the foreigners he had shown cowardice. In his place, he would have thwarted their haughtiness.

Author's husband King and brothers-in-law Sin and Tee.

In Hong Kong, Big Brother was invited to a party given by Uncle Peck's father-in-law. Every literary man in town was present. A scholarly discussion on the Tang and Sung masters was to be held. There were a number of prominent poets in the party and Big Brother was proud to be asked to contribute his latest poem. When he returned to the steamer, he told Mr. Lee of the honour he had been given at the party. Mr. Lee kept silent. All these pompous things did not impress him in the least. For him, only reality counted. He told me that as a boy, he used to ride home on a buffalo after a day's laborious work.

'You see, the buffalo was our sole bread-winner.'

I realised then that he and Big Brother were of two different worlds. His was a planet rising slowly into orbit but once broken through, it shone in all its splendour while Big Brother's star eclipsed only too soon.

We basked in Mr. Lee's company for the rest of the voyage to Singapore. We delighted in his wit and inexhaustible sense of humour. But although we asked him to join us in the dining room, he never accepted our invitation. He told us in his pragmatic way: 'I get the same in the second class.'

However, at other times we found him in our window seat waiting for us with tea prepared by Ming-hsian. This he could never refuse. I had the feeling that he enjoyed being with us as much as we with him.

2

Urine saves little sister Nonie's life

PAPA AND MAMA were waiting on the quay with the little brothers and sister. I waved frantically with my handkerchief to attract their attention. As soon as the steamer docked, everybody scrambled on deck. Papa walked towards us looking as if he did not recognize me. I called out to him, but his trembling lips found no words for his homecoming daughter. He turned instead to welcome his son-in-law. Mama was undemonstrative. She hardly gave me a glance and joined Papa in conversation with Big Brother. I was the point of interest only to my brothers, who wanted to know whether I had brought them toys.

The Sultan's private coach, which two years before sent us on our trip to China, brought us back to Medan where a large section of the Hakka and Hokkien community had gathered at the station to greet the son-in-law of their Chief. Through our union, the former antagonism that existed between these two dialect groups had come to an end. For weeks, we attended numerous dinner parties where Big Brother was the guest of honour and was feted according to old customs.

I, on the other hand, kept myself busy with acquiring a new wardrobe. I had become so thin that most of my clothes did not fit, and Mama was disgusted with my poor taste.

One day, after shopping and calling on old friends, Mama decided to show off my little sister's talent. Though she was hardly four, she could sing and play the piano very well. Although the Big House was under repair at that time, Mama took us to the grand piano which stood in the ballroom. How well I remembered the interminable scales I used to play on it. And now from my little sister's dainty and nimble fingers, a sweet melody reached our ears. After the performance she bowed at our applause and silently walked to the window to watch the passers-by in the street below. Then I was asked by Mrs. Baay, the piano teacher to demonstrate my musical achievements acquired under the tutelage of Maestro Paci. But it proved to be a poor show because I had not touched a key since my marriage.

When I had finished my piece, someone noticed that my little sister had disappeared. Mama ran to the window, let out a piercing scream and made for the stairs.

Mama was clutching my little sister tightly to her breast when we got to the courtyard. A crowd had gathered and we heard people who saw the fall say that she fell first on the tiled awning under the balcony and then to the ground. The break in the fall had probably saved her life.

Mama carried my little sister inside the house and Dr. van Hengel arrived soon after. Nonie was motionless, lying limply in Mama's arms and breathing evenly as if in a deep sleep. After examining my little sister, the doctor declared that nothing was broken. Yet nothing could revive her. Then suddenly, a voice said: 'Urine, quick! Urine of a boy.' It was Aunt Hsi, Uncle Yong-hian's widow who, coming from the village, knew only the ancient methods. Someone came with a teacup of urine. Aunt Hsi opened my little sister's mouth with her finger and poured a few drops in, slowly another few drops went down the little girl's throat. She began to move and slowly opened her eyes.

'Where's my doll?' she asked.

Dr. van Hengel could hardly believe his eyes. Papa lit candles and joss-sticks in the ancestral hall to thank God and the ancestors for having restored Nonie's life.

We went back to the country house and immediately told Big Brother what had happened. He was very shocked upon hearing about the fall but was amazed at the miraculous recovery. Papa said to him: 'Your wife had just begun to put on a bit of weight and a little colour, why must she be given such a fright!'

Mama looked at Papa, her eyes flashing but in Papa's I noticed unmistakable tears. He was concerned about my health. Poor Papa.

3

Bandar Baroe — serenity's abode

A MONTH PASSED without our realising it. Big Brother often called upon my cousin Pu-ching (Uncle Yong-hian's son) and cousin-in-law Kun-kok. Both were scholars in the Chinese classics and so they had much in common. Everything was going smoothly. We were having a wonderful time.

One day, we received a letter from my father-in-law saying that Eighth Grandmother, Uncle Peck's mother, had passed away from a stroke. At the same time, there had been a fire in our old rooms where many of our things, including the two Chinese leather suitcases with the gold ornaments used at my wedding, were stored. The suitcases were totally destroyed and the gold gone. To console me, my father-in-law promised to restitute my loss in good time. It never happened and I never asked.

After the news of the calamities, we did not prolong our visit. Papa quite agreed that we should go home to be with the elders in their misfortune. I began to realise that now home meant the home of my parents-in-law and that in my parents' home, I was a mere guest.

Two weeks later, we departed and arrived in Amoy just before Chinese New Year. We stayed with Mother-in-law in the Big House. How my son Tong had grown. In the few months we were away he had become the fattest baby in Amoy. He was so heavy that I could never carry him for more than a few minutes. He was just learning to crawl and would chortle with delight when his wet-nurse Han-ah approached, swaying on her bound feet, for his feed.

When autumn neared, my parents-in-law finding that Big Brother's health fared better in a tropical climate, sent us again to Medan but this time for as long as we wished.

Of course my parents were delighted to have us — especially my father.

Papa took us to Bandar Baroe where he had a tea plantation. We stayed in a lovely bungalow which was built on stilts, with an attap roof. By the side there was a merry little stream. From the back we could see a magnificent mountain range that seemed to magnify the beauty of the roses and dahlias that grew abundantly in the garden. It was indeed a picturesque abode. Big Brother was exhilarated. This was his idea of peace and serenity.

And it was here that he was inspired to write his first volume of poems of the Batak lands.

We spent much of our time reading and studying. My knowledge of Chinese literature had improved considerably. I was encouraged to compose my first poem which I titled 'A Rose'. My husband thought my style simple, yet expressive and sincere. I was more than pleased.

Those idyllic days went past at a leisurely pace. The serene surroundings made us forget time. We were both putting on weight and instead of two weeks, we stayed for a whole month.

4

'Our poor friend'
— the rubber magnate

MR. LEE KONG CHIAN, true to his words, visited us. Big Brother took him to meet Papa on whom our friend made a most favourable impression. Papa asked Big Brother to show him around.

They went first of all to the Deli Bank where Big Brother pointed out that it had been founded by my father and some of his old friends including Tio Tiauw-set, Papa's original benefactor. At that time, the bank could already be compared with the foreign banks in the city. It had all the Chinese clientele. The Bank's building was far from conspicuous; the site was but two shophouses facing the old fish market. In spite of the growing business, the shareholders, maintaining their superstitious belief in *Fung Shui* (a Chinese geomantic system by means of which sites are determined propitious for houses, buildings, businesses and graves), obstinately kept the bank to its modest appearance.

The Chinese Club 'Yan Khin Hian' appealed little to Mr. Lee when he saw prosperous pot-bellied businessmen squandering money in gambling, drink and song. However, he praised the charitable work of the Chinese hospital Tjie On Jie Jan and was impressed by the temples and the Kwantung graveyard. The next day, they visited Si Boelan, my father's first plantation which now had grown into a big concern with numerous rubber estates. There was no time to go to the coconut plantations.

'Well,' said Mr. Lee, 'it looks as if the whole of Medan belongs to your father-in-law! And his rubber enterprises.... It shouldn't be difficult for you to start something yourself.'

'If my father-in-law could achieve all this, why can't I?' Big Brother responded confidently as if they were discussing a matter of fact.

'Your father-in-law started from the bottom. He's a self-made man. He knows what hardship means while you were born with the silver spoon in your mouth.'

'Yes, but things are different now and it would be easier for me even without his influence. One had only to command,' Big Brother retorted.

'You'll be surprised, Big Brother. Don't be over ambitious,' Mr. Lee replied earnestly.

Papa had offered Mr. Lee a scholarship to the Hong Kong University. But when he returned to Singapore, Mr. Lee wrote to Big Brother that he had taken up an offer of a job in a shoe factory. It was owned by Tan Kah Kee.

Mr. Lee Kong Chian (Photo by kind permission of Mr. Lee Seng Gee).

Not long after, the urge for travelling took us to Singapore. We wanted to pay Mr. Lee a return visit. As soon as we had taken dinner at the Europe Hotel, we hailed a taxi and told the driver to take us to the address Mr. Lee had given in his letter. It was evening and as we were not familiar with the location we asked the driver whether he was sure that we were at the right address.

'Where could it be if not here?' he answered roughly. 'Any child would know the Tan Kah Kee Rubber Shoe Factory because everybody is wearing their shoes.'

Hesitantly, Big Brother knocked on the old-fashioned Chinese wooden door.

We heard the shuffling and moving of furniture and then the removing of the wooden bolt which kept the door locked. In the half-light, our friend appeared in shorts and a sleeveless singlet. He grinned broadly and was genuinely pleased to see us. He led us inside a small square room where there was a camp bed, a table and a chair.

'Were you asleep already?' asked Big Brother.

'Yes, on the camp bed pushed against the door to protect myself from unexpected intruders like you,' he teased.

'You live here? With all the smell of rubber around you?' Big Brother said incredulously.

'It is part of my job. I start at the bottom,' Mr. Lee explained good naturedly, 'how different it is from Hong Kong University. However, I'm not complaining.'

After a brief chat, Mr. Lee said that he had to rest for work in the morning and regretted not being able to keep us company. But he promised to come to see us as soon as he could.

With his promise, we said our goodnights and returned to our hotel. In the car, Big Brother gave a deep sigh.

'Our poor friend,' he said sympathetically.

Who was to foresee that the 'poor friend' was to become a rubber magnate!

〜※〜

5

'You see, Brother Lee, the King of Hades doesn't need me yet'

A WEEK PASSED. I enjoyed shopping in the numerous Chinese and Indian shops near the Lane Crawford departmental store. In the afternoon, we sat on the hotel veranda taking our habitual 4 o'clock tea and watching tennis and cricket being played on the Padang just across the road. Along the Esplanade, pedestrians enjoyed the cool sea breeze and watched ocean-going steamers and an assortment of native vessels sail by. This was the routine in the evenings in the port of Singapore.

Big Brother had made the acquaintance of several foreigners staying at the hotel, among whom was a representative of Palmolive Soap Company who had offered him the agency in Medan. Big Brother was now contemplating business seriously. Accompanied by his cousin Teng-hua he called on the local businessmen, the majority from Chiang-chiu and Chuan-chiu. They were only too pleased to enter into business connections with such a distinguished person — the eldest son of the Lim family of Amoy and Taiwan and, at the same time, son-in-law of Medan's Tjong A Fie. According to Chinese customs, the prelude to business talks were dinner parties. Big Brother was invited to many but I was automatically excluded because at such dinner parties, sing-song girls were present to serve wine.

We made two social calls together. One was to Mr. Tan Kah Kee who was no stranger to the Lim family and who received us well. Knowing that Big Brother was no businessman, he told him, among other things, of his own intention to retire from business and devote himself to educational work. The other was to Dr. Lim Boon Keng and his wife whom we knew in Kulangsu when they were invited to officiate as go-between at our wedding ceremony in Amoy (in lieu of our actual matchmaker Lim Lai-sang who had left us in Hong Kong).

One day, returning from a luncheon party with his cousin, Big Brother felt rather tired and later complained of belly-ache. 'It must be indigestion from the food I've taken at lunch,' he said, 'give me a dose of Eno fruit salt.'

After that, he fell asleep only to be awakened by spasms of greater pain. Ming-hsian brought him a hot water bottle but it did not help. Then we sent for the hotel doctor. He advised us to take Big Brother to the General Hospital. He might need an operation. It was already nine in the evening. I protested and demanded that we first consult our friend Dr. Lim Boon Keng. Dr. Lim came immediately and stated the same thing.

'How do I dare take such a grave responsibility?' I cried desperately, 'we must ask his parents first.'

'I don't think we have time to waste,' Dr. Lim said decisively, 'the operation is most urgent.' And changing to a milder tone, he said: 'I shall bring him to the hospital myself. Come with me.'

In the meantime, Big Brother was writhing and moaning on his bed. His fists were clenched and knees bent, rolling himself into a ball. In this pitiful condition, they carried him to the car. Big Brother lay with his head on my lap, his eyes closed, his mouth open, murmuring incoherent words.

At the hospital I had to sign a paper consenting to the operation and Big Brother was wheeled into the operation room. I had not even a chance to say a word of encouragement to him.

'Don't be afraid, Dr. Smith is the best surgeon we have in Singapore.' Dr. Lim touched me sympathetically on the shoulder. I cried without restraint....

I don't know how long I had been sitting outside the operating room. The hours seemed forever. Though anguished, not the slightest thought entered my mind that my husband might die.

Then a door opened, and an Indian assistant came out, his white dress spattered with blood. I closed my eyes. I thought I was going to faint. I heard someone saying: 'Thank God, he has survived!' Suddenly I felt very tired.

I was given a drink. I sipped a little. It was bitter. Then slowly I opened my eyes. I was aware of intense activity around me and found Dr. Lim Boon Keng holding my hand. He smiled kindly.

'Your husband is alright but it was a serious operation. With an ordinary appendicitis it would have been simple but the young gentleman had waited too long. It was peritonitis. They've made five holes to drain out all the poison.'

'But he never complained about his stomach before. What his parents had been afraid of was his chest,' I said.

Every morning and afternoon, I was allowed to see him for an hour at a time. There were two nurses, a day nurse and a night nurse to look after him. The faithful valet, Ming-hsian, volunteered to sleep at the hospital for the first week until his master was out of danger. No expenses were spared and Dr. Lim Boon Keng had taken the responsibility of informing my parents-in-law of the successful operation.

I received a letter from them advising me not to upset Big Brother under any circumstances whatsoever and let him enjoy anything he wished at his lucky 'rebirth'. I sighed with relief for not having been blamed for taking matters into my own hands. What would have happened had the operation turned out otherwise? I shivered at the thought of it.

Mr. Lee came at once after he was told of Big Brother's escape from death by Dr. Lim. He just stood there without speaking; his usual good humour had deserted him on seeing his friend in such a state.

Big Brother smiled wanly and said: 'You see, Brother Lee, the King of Hades doesn't need me yet.' .

6

Queeny meets 'the other woman'

BIG BROTHER'S RECOVERY was satisfactory and, as recommended by his doctors, we decided to rent a seaside bungalow for his recuperation. So, after his discharge from hospital, we settled down in the Bedok bungalow belonging to a prominent Teochew businessman in Singapore. (Coincidentally, many, many years later we became related to the family by marriage. Brother Fa-liong's eldest daughter was married to one of his grandsons, Seah Peng Ee.) Gradually, accompanied by his cousin Teng-hua, Big Brother resumed his association with his newly acquired friends; he was still interested in business.

Mr. Lee had called twice to find out how Big Brother was spending his time. However, he made no comment when told of Big Brother's interest in business.

One day, I received a bill from Lane Crawford for two ladies' watches which I had never bought. When Big Brother returned from his calls, I showed him the bill.

'Oh,' he drawled, 'I thought you might want to give a little present to the two nurses who looked after me.'

I wanted to ask why the bill was addressed to me but kept silent. Thus, I came to realise that my husband was giving away presents to other women without my knowledge.

On one occasion, cousin Teng-hua returned alone after having dined in town with Big Brother.

'Where's Big Brother?' I asked.

'He'll be back later,' he replied, seemingly embarrassed.

'Why are you not with him?' his wife asked.

'Well, Big Brother told me to come home first. He went to the house of a friend.'

'What friend?' I insisted. Then the truth came out. Big Brother had become infatuated with a young sing-song girl. I had heard about these stag parties where each gentleman had his favourite girl sit by his side to serve him wine, but thought nothing of it. But at this information I was upset. So, Big Brother also had his favourite.

'How long has this been going on?' I questioned Teng-hua.

'About a week or so but it seems that Big Brother has become very attached to the girl.'

'Well, bring the girl to me tomorrow.'

'But ...'

'No buts. I want to see her.'

Nothing was mentioned when Big Brother came home after midnight.

The following morning, Teng-hua brought the sing-song girl to the bungalow. Big Brother looked a fool with his mouth agape. The girl greeted me respectfully and said: 'It's very kind of you to invite me to lunch.'

I noticed she had nice manners but they were of the 'green house' school (name for brothels): she was about seventeen years of age with nice features and a graceful figure.

We all sat down on the veranda facing the sea. Ming-hsian served tea. Big Brother was most uncomfortable and spilled his drink.

'I've asked you to come,' I began, 'to tell you to come with me to Medan. Would you like it?'

'Oh, certainly, I shall be honoured to visit your illustrious home.'

'As you're my husband's friend, you will be mine also. Please make yourself at home here, don't stand on ceremony,' I finished with the most amiable smile. No one suspected what was to follow. After lunch, the girl took leave with profuse thanks.

'Move your things here tomorrow, we're returning to Medan in a few days' time,' I urged. The girl nodded lamely, looking at Big Brother who averted his gaze.

The next day, the girl did not appear. I sent Teng-huá for her but he came back alone.

'The girl is scared beyond belief. She said if she took you at your word and went with you to Medan where your father is king, she would be skinned alive and then cooked in a cauldron.'

I laughed.

'That wasn't my intention at all. I wanted to see whether she can endure an austere life in exchange for the gaieties she's used to. Besides, haven't my parents-in-law ordered me to let Big Brother enjoy whatever he fancies after his "rebirth"? If you ever meet her again, tell her that I never bore such murderous thoughts.'

Big Brother's affair ended then and there.

7

Big Brother's miraculous 'rebirth' is applauded; a beautiful surprise

AT THE END of the year we returned to Amoy for the Chinese New Year. Our arrival caused a big stir and commotion in the household. All the relatives and friends came one after the other, congratulating my parents-in-law on their eldest son's 'rebirth'. The most touching of all was Mother-in-law who seldom displayed her emotions, but now talked and laughed through her tears which she could hardly control. For a whole month, members of the family prepared palatable dishes to satisfy Big Brother's greedy appetite. Having never seen him eat with so much relish, Mother-in-law just sat there by his side watching. Although a happy smile played on her lips, there was fear in her soft eyes that she might lose this son again. The ordeal he had suffered was told and retold until it almost became a legend. I stood by silently throughout as not a question was put to me concerning the episode. Sometimes, I was even met with murderous glares from women who thought me more barbaric than ever. As if I had been the 'butcher'! Big Brother delighted in his importance and, to draw more sympathy, never discarded his cane on which he leant heavily, though he could walk as well as any healthy man. When I asked him, he replied with a grin: 'You see how stupid these ignorant people are!'

I was most relieved when life became normal again without someone lurking around just to have a glimpse of the 'reborn'.

In the meantime, we received a telegram from my father saying that I had a new little brother born on the same day as the famous noble warrior of the Three Kingdoms, Kwan Kung. Just imagine, a little brother, younger than my own son! Not long after, my mother wrote that my father was to celebrate his thirty years' service with the Dutch Government and wanted his family near and far to attend. He would pay all the expenses for those who came from his village.

On the day of our arrival, when we greeted my father, he took a blue velvet case from his pocket. He opened it and revealed a wonderful necklace of fourteen diamonds. Each was crafted into a flower. They were perfectly matched and about four to five carats each. Papa put it round my neck as I caressed it softly.

'It feels so cool and refreshing, just like the fresh morning dew,' I murmured, my eyes brimming with tears.

'Why do you cry child? Don't you like it?' my father asked anxiously.

'Oh. Papa. I'm overwhelmingly happy; never in my life shall I wish for anything else!'

8

Papa's moment of triumph

PAPA CELEBRATED HIS jubilee in 1916. The day of the jubilee began with a fanfare of cymbals, drums and firecrackers. From Hong Kong Street across the railway track came a procession of lion dancers prancing joyously. It stopped in front of our house. A delegate in festive clothes walked into the front hall, presenting a big red card on a silver plate. It was the emissary of the Chinese community who offered their congratulations on this great day. The 'lion' recently ordered from China danced in the direction of the ancestral hall, bowed three times then retreated to the front yard to give a performance. We admired the new costumes and the gleaming weapons of the boxers. It was like New Year.

There was no end of visitors. With each, Papa and Mama had to pose for pictures until at last it got so much on Mama's nerves that in most of them she showed more a sour than a smiling face. Besides her duty as hostess, she had also the duty of a mother. Every three hours she had to undress and feed her baby before dressing up anew in the heat of the day.

There were processions and floats portraying scenes from ancient history of various knights and beautiful women. The main street of Kewawan was so filled with crowds that the traffic had to be directed to other routes. Respite came only with the midday meal. Then it started again. In the evening, the streets were lit like fairyland and there were fireworks on the Esplanade. The Indian shops along the main street did their share in decorating their facades, with each one attempting to surpass the other. In the Chinese section, the streets were even more packed and Yan Khin Hian, the Chinese Club, remained

Father and Mother on his jubilee, 1916.

Group photograph taken at Father's jubilee.

open all night. The programme consisted of a whole week of recreation and enjoyment. The mornings were occupied with visits from the different communities: Arabs, Indians, Sikhs and Malays came in national attire to pay their respects. Then there were delegates from the various associations. School children from the different towns enjoyed a free ride in the train to come to Medan to attend the celebrations. It was a holiday for everybody. The populace remembered well all Tjong A Fie had done for the people of all races and their spontaneous tributes were most gratifying. It was as if everyone wanted to honour the great man in recognition of his justice and charity.

The last day of the festivities was specially planned for the European community. In the afternoon, a fancy dress party for children was attended by more than five hundred boys and

Author, little sister Sze-yin, and brothers
Kian-liong and Kwet-liong in fancy dress.

girls of all ages.

That evening there was to be a ball. A Dutch couple who were professional dancers were invited to give performances of the latest dances, the Fox-trot and Tango, then in vogue in Europe. Champagne flowed in abundance and the sound of popping corks continued till the small hours of the morning.

At the ball I wore an aquamarine chiffon dress, very simple in cut, made by my dear Aunt Duson, to match my necklace. The combination was perfect and gave me a fairy-like appearance, with the diamonds sparkling in the bright lights. I was admired by many young men who guarded themselves against reaching for the forbidden fruit because my parents, knowing their foreign manners, followed me with their eyes to intercept possible flirtations. Big Brother however was aloof, apparently regarding my success as a compliment. When the signal was given for the Cotillion, Big Brother disappeared. Luckily, Helling, an employee of Uncle Onnes came to my rescue. After the dance, he escorted me to the long table where the ladies were choosing their presents. Helling took a delicate Delft porcelain vase and offered it to me.

'Thank you, but don't you have a favourite lady to give it to?' I asked.

'My bride is coming out from Holland next year when I can afford to get married,' he smiled.

'And my husband is already dreaming in his cot; he doesn't like dancing and prefers his books. He's a scholar.' I laughed.

'He seems very intelligent to me. I had a long talk with him earlier in the evening. He's interested in business.' Helling commented.

I smiled and we followed the crowd back to the ballroom.

When we said our goodnights (or rather good mornings) to the guests, Papa stood erect, watching with great amusement as the last of them stumbled into their cars or somebody else's.

'I'm glad they feel happy,' he said, considering himself champion of even the best drinkers.

It had indeed been a triumphant day for my father.

Part Four

1

Great-uncle Tio Tiauw-set

MY FATHER HAD received a cable from Batavia (now Jakarta) that his old friend Tio Tiauw-set had suddenly died of a heart attack. He was distressed beyond words. He mourned him not only as a very dear friend but also as his benefactor who took him in when he first arrived from the village as a *singkeh* (newcomer). Encouraged by the old pioneer, my father, in his thirty years of assiduous work from eight in the morning till eight in the evening with only an hour's break for lunch, had achieved his great ambition to prove to his village people that he could be successful. Sometimes, after dinner he would return again to his office and work till after midnight which infuriated my mother who would put all the blame on great-uncle Tiauw-set for his influence on his protege. But my father merely smiled when my mother stormed at him that he might just as well imitate his friend and have a harem too; for it was true that Tio Tiauw-set, whose wife had died after the birth of their daughter, had acquired one concubine after another but he had never remarried for the sake of his daughter who was very dear to him.

Although Tio Tiauw-set was gone, a legend survived him. It tells of how Tio Tiauw-set, from a very poor cowherd in Tai Poo, became one of the richest men in Penang. Sailing in the big wooden junk, he arrived first on the shores of Java. In Batavia, he was employed as water carrier by the owner of a sundry shop. Advised by his employer that *singkehs* must bathe three times a day to avoid the fever, he bathed in the river running under the house. He usually sat on a hump-like stone, washing and scrubbing himself. The sundry shop owner's daughter, who was already of marriageable age, often cast side-glances at the handsome *singkeh*. When matchmakers came to ask her parents for her hand, the daughter refused their proposals obstinately and as she was their only child, the elders did not press her. They were only too glad to have her with them awaiting to pick out a worthy son-in-law. As time passed, the daughter at last admitted her secret love for the water carrier. Though reluctant to let her marry a *singkeh*, the parents gave in to their beloved child's wish. As the water carrier was an ardent worker and often helped in the shop itself, the prospective father-in-law overlooked all other obstacles and gave Tiauw-set money to start a business of his own. In this capacity, he was fit to marry the daughter of the house. One night, seeking his bath at the usual spot, he found his bathing stone gone. It was later discovered that the hump was no stone at all but the back of an old crocodile.

Thus goes the legend that even a crocodile has the sense to spare the life of a great man.

Great-uncle Tiauw-set had named my father sole executor of his will and he therefore had to go to Batavia immediately. He decided to take my mother, little baby Lee-liong, my husband and I along and thus the next day, we boarded the K.P.M. steamer *Ophir* for Java.

Great-uncle Tio Tiauw-set.

It was my father's first visit to the capital. He was met at the quay by several well-known families of the Hakka clan and compatriots of his village in Meishien. They were elated to meet, at last, the man whose name was on everyone's lips for the past decade.

In the house of mourning we met great-uncle Tiauw-set's fourth concubine with her adopted son Pin-liong, and his seventh concubine with her two little sons who were born when great-uncle was already nearing his seventies. It was not an easy job for my father to please the widows who both wanted to occupy the place of precedency. After a fortnight of meetings, discussions and quarrels between the two concubines, my father finally arrived at a satisfactory compromise. When the whole matter came to a close, he thought it proper to make courtesy calls on the local Chinese chiefs, his contemporaries: Major Koh Kim-an, Captain Lie Tjien-tjoen and Koo Ah-fan. They welcomed my father with great enthusiasm having heard of his work and deeds in Sumatra. It was at this time that my father made known that it was his late friend's wish to establish a Chinese bank in Batavia as he and my father had done in Medan. The prospect was warmly received and after several discussions Major Koh Kim-an and Captain Lie Tjien-tjoen promised to go to Medan to finalise arrangements.

Two weeks later, the Batavian party arrived in Medan. They were royally entertained at dinners and luncheons and made trips to the Si Boelan and Tandjoeng Poetri companies visiting coconut, coffee and tea plantations. We even took them to visit the Lepers Colony at Poeloe Sitjanang which was built with the contributions of my father.

Before they left for home, Major Koh Kim-an's party signed the Batavia Bank's contract. My father was allotted two hundred shares out of the six hundred. Major Koh, Captain Lie and his brother-in law held the remaining shares. Thus my father had expanded his business to the neighbouring island as well.

2

Queeny — propitious wife

AS MY FATHER'S vast business concerns were still expanding, he saw to it that each of his sons-in-law were put in charge of one of these interests. My husband was made manager of the Deli Bank in Medan and we were given a house of our own in the elite quarters of the city.

When we had moved to our new home, we were free to do as we pleased, being no longer under the surveillance of my mother's sharp eyes.

We sent for Ah-gong, our fabulous cook and my maid, Hoon-ah. Together they saw to the domestic duties of our home. I was, as of old, horribly weak in this area and was content just to see that a pleasant atmosphere was maintained at home. Ming-hsian, the trusted valet was promoted to butler. He was now in charge of the daily running of the household and I left things entirely in his hands, including expenditure.

Our new home was an old fashioned wooden bungalow built on stone pillars and encircled by open verandas. A short flight of cement steps led to the front veranda appointed with rattan matting and cane furniture. Potted plants and ferns gave it a cosy atmosphere. Inside, the sitting room was dominated by an upholstered settee and an upright piano. On the left was my boudoir where I entertained only the most intimate friends. On the other side of the sitting room was our bedroom and dressing area. Wooden stairs led from the back of the house to the kitchen, storeroom, bath and toilet. There was also a small pavilion and servant quarters.

One day we gave a garden party with an authentic Hawaiian band from Hawaii. We invited only the younger

Our first house in Medan.

set. The highest position held by the young men was but that of proxy or department chief of banks or big business concerns. We were too young to move in the circle of older executives. My father came by to see whom we had assembled and seemed pleased with our choice of friends. It was a very successful party and on this occasion we strengthened our friendship with the Reuvers: Minnie and Sup, who was then at the Kehding and Company. Wim van Oyen, second man in the Nederlandsche Handelmaatschappij (Netherlands Trading Co.) was also there. So were the Hellings of the Kamerligh Onnes administration office and the Abersons, a lawyer and his wife who was my schoolmate. There were many others but none as loyal as the Reuvers (Minnie died in 1976 but I still correspond with Sup who is living in New York). Although I had never met Noes van Oyen, she wrote to me after Wim, her husband, died that she would like to continue the longstanding friendship. I met her for the first time in Holland in 1974 although I already knew her sons Wim and Frits and their wives.

My husband seemed to be absorbed in his new appoint-ment, leaving no time for his scholarly work. He went regularly to the Deli Bank at eight in the morning, came home for lunch and after a short nap, was there again from two to five. Our life ran like a clock.

The first thing my husband did with the money he earned was to buy a present for his mother. When we went to Amoy for the Chinese New Year, he laid before her a blue velvet box containing a diamond *kerungsang*. My mother-in-law was delighted.

Big Brother was now regarded with deep respect. Unlike the year before when he had been condoled for his serious operation, he now was acclaimed a moneymaking phenomenon. Such are human beings! Even I had risen in their esteem; I was no more considered a barbarian but a propitious wife bringing luck to the husband.

3

Little Tong and his grandmother

MY MOTHER-IN-LAW had allowed little Tong to stay with us. He was now nearly three years old and we hoped that we could take our son with us to show him to his maternal grandparents.

One afternoon, Han-ah, Tong's nurse came in with a bowl of vermicelli soup. On seeing this, Tong got up from where he was playing and tugged at the nurse's sleeve. The bowl of hot soup was spilled on the little boy's throat. My scream brought my husband and his friends from the other room where they were playing *mahjong*. Everybody was gesticulating and advising that pork fat should be applied on the blisters which had rapidly appeared. I did not know what to do. What would my mother-in-law say when she heard about this? And sure enough, she was promptly informed by one of the servants who went to the Big House for pork fat.

She stumbled up the stone steps, supported by two servant girls, crying without restraint: 'Oh, my pet, my precious, my heart of hearts, what have they done to you!'

'It was an accident, mother,' explained my husband, 'don't be alarmed. It's alright. Please sit down and rest yourself.'

'Sit down?' she demonstrated with scorn. 'I left my little one in your care just to see whether you could look after him as I had done and now this happens to him. I won't leave him here another minute.'

Little Tong, who had not cried throughout the whole incident, walked over to his grandmother. He sought her hand and held it tightly with his little fingers as if to assure her that he was alright.

Little Tong (3 years old).

My mother-in-law stood up. Without another word she and my son walked down the stone steps back into the Big House.

That ended our aspiration to have our son with us in Medan and we never mentioned it again. We returned to Medan without Tong. I regretted all my life that my father had not seen my little son. Things would have been different, perhaps. And all that happened later might not have happened at all…

***

My mother was suffering from an inflammation of the eyes and fearing the worst, my father had arranged for Uncle Chooi-lye, mother's second brother, my husband and I to accompany her to Bandoeng in Java to see an eye specialist.

We stayed at the chic Hotel Homann with the best European food, cooked under the supervision of a French chef. Everyday, the three of us took turns to go with my mother to the doctor's clinic where she was treated for ophthalmia. After three weeks, she was allowed to go home on the condition that she came back in six months' time for a check-up. We felt relieved and happy and before leaving Bandoeng, we made a trip to Garoet, a mountain resort. The scenery was beautiful and the climate cooler than Bandoeng. We heard that they made the most beautiful hand-painted sarongs there. My mother bought a few.

When we reached home, my mother handed my father a cheque which she had received from Uncle Chooi-lye who was in charge of the expenses for the trip. 'I didn't use the money,' she said.

'What?' my father was astonished. 'You didn't buy any jewellery? I had seen the diamond on Major Koh Kim-an's wife and thought you might want one just like hers.'

'I'm quite satisfied with all that you've given me,' she answered, smiling happily.

For all that she was, arrogant, stubborn, spoilt and uncontrollable, my mother was not greedy.

4

The catastrophe

A FEW WEEKS later, my father received a visit from one of his business associates from Penang, Mr. Koo Han-liong. As he had expressly wanted to look at the rubber estates, a trip to Si Boelan was fixed for Sunday with another of my father's friend from Medan, Uncle Oei Soei-hoe.

Unfortunately, that Sunday, the driver fell ill but his assistant said that he could drive the car. They left early in the morning, the two gentlemen at the back and my father in front next to the chauffeur.

Two hours later, a telephone call came from Simpang Tiga. The caller said that my father had met with an accident. The chauffeur in avoiding a *sado* has lost control of the car and had run against a water pump on the side of the road. My father and his friends were taken to the hospital at Simpang Tiga. As my mother was at the time resting in Poeloe Brayan because of her eyes, I left my husband to notify his mother-in-law and hurriedly set off for Simpang Tiga alone. Throughout the long lonely journey, horrible thoughts ran through my head: perhaps I would see my father bathed in blood with broken legs and arms or perhaps... dead!

When I stepped out of the car, my knees were trembling, I could hardly walk. Then I saw my father. He was sitting all alone in a rattan chair in the waiting room of the hospital. I staggered to him and clutched his arm.

Falling to my knees beside his chair, I sobbed uncontrollably.

My father was shaking with emotion. Eventually he said gently: 'Now, now,' patting my head softly, 'get up and don't cry. Your father's alright.'

I got up, then noticed scratches on his face and hands. Before I could say anything, Uncle Soei-hoe came into the room.

'Don't cry, my girl, your father is fortunate to have escaped with nothing but a few scratches,' he said, reassuringly.

'But Uncle, you've hurt your head!"

'Oh, that's nothing. The doctor just wanted to put a bandage around it. It's just a slight wound,' he said.

'How's our friend?' my father asked anxiously.

'He's in a bad state,' Uncle Soei-hoe answered. 'The doctor said that the injured leg might have to be amputated. He's afraid of gangrene. I've already cabled his son in Penang. Let's go back to Medan now. Brother Koo will follow later in an ambulance.'

My father made a movement to go to the casualty room where Mr. Koo Han-liong had been taken but Uncle Soei-hoe stopped him saying: 'You won't be able to talk to him at this moment, he's under sedation.'

We left the hospital in my car, and I told the driver to go at a moderate speed.

After we had sent Uncle Soei-hoe home, we returned to the Big House where we found my mother worshipping at the ancestors' altar and before the God of Heaven. My father did not utter a word, perhaps he was overcome with emotion. He just shook his head and went straight to his room to wash up. We were very quiet that day, obviously shaken by the day's events.

The next day, Mrs. Koo and her eldest son arrived from Penang. They went straight to the Deli Hospital where they held a conference with the doctors and my father. It was gloomy awaiting news from the hospital. On the third day, we were informed that Mr. Koo Han-liong had succumbed during his third operation. Before his death he had reiterated to his wife and son never to blame my father for the accident.

Three days later, a telegram arrived from Singapore. Uncle Soei-hoe had suddenly died there after attending a party. He had diabetes. The cause of death was the slight wound on his head. Such are the ways of Fate in which we mortals are helpless.

Discipline and Tjong A Fie

ONE WEEKEND, in Bandar Baroe, the tea plantation, I noticed a young Javanese woman working in the field. I asked Mr. Siemssen the manager whether I could employ her.

'I'm sorry,' he replied, 'she's a contract coolie and is not able to work elsewhere until her contract with the estate expires.'

'But I want to have her,' I pouted.

'Then you should ask your father,' Mr. Siemssen suggested.

So, when I saw Papa at lunchtime the following day, I asked him about the Javanese woman.

'Of course you can have her,' he answered without any hesitation.

He telephoned Mr. Siemssen and the next day Moersinah was at our house, to the great annoyance of my mother who resented my father never having refused me anything.

'To spoil her like that,' she snorted, 'what about my son? You have never granted him anything.'

'I think it is enough that only one of us spoils him. I am not ignorant of the fact that you scold everybody who dares to mention anything wayward about him. You let him have a car though he hasn't reached the age of eighteen. You can't even control where he's going or know what kind of company he keeps.'

That's for you to find out. Don't you have your trusted *tjintengs* (bodyguards)'!'

'If I used them on your son, you'll have the audacity to dismiss them and humble me. In any case, I'm not going to put a detective on the track of my own son. I trust he's not doing anything wrong.'

'He's still young,' my mother said defensively.

'When I was his age, I was already looking after my father's shop and the family.'

'Don't compare him with yourself.'

'The boy must learn discipline, how can he otherwise succeed me? You remember last year when he had that accident with his car? The police took his number and served a summons on him. Of course the matter could have been settled amicably but I insisted that he must go to court to prove himself innocent. After the investigations, it came out that it wasn't Fa-liong's fault at all. So he was innocent and nobody could say that Tjong A Fie put pressure on the law.'

'You would have allowed your son to be sent to prison?' retorted my mother hotly.

'That's discipline. Haven't I been right? I wish that you...'

'Stop! I don't want to hear another word,' my mother cried furiously.

Just at that moment, the clock struck two. My father took his cap and walked through the front door to his office.

After consulting Uncle Onnes, my father decided that it was best that Fa-liong be sent to Japan. My mother had protested half-heartedly. She knew that my father was right. Fa-liong was at a vulnerable age, easily corrupted by the lavish company he mixed with. Onnes was to go with him. So were my husband and I.

'But what about his marriage?' my mother tried weakly, hoping to keep her son.

Fa-liong was to marry my husband's third sister, Hong-hiong. Third Sister was the least educated in the Chinese classics and her conduct less refined than that of her sisters. She was the one who corrected the numerous servant girls when they stepped out of line. Sitting in a tall chair with a feather duster in her hand, she would lecture them on their duties and scold them for their faults. She would even administer strokes with the duster. This, the elder sisters abhorred to do themselves. Therefore, Third Sister gained the nickname of 'hero'. So when the marriage proposal came through her elder brother, the family accepted it without a thought. They deemed her most eligible for the barbarian country where the one-eyed man is king.

I advised strongly against it, knowing my mother's unpredictable character. I also feared being involved in family disputes which would surely arise between in-laws resulting from such a union. My husband philosophically left everything to Fate.

6

A tyrannous mother-in-law

IT WAS DECIDED that Fa-liong and Third Sister were to be married in Kobe, Japan. Mr. Ong Keng Siong, Ghee's father-in-law and a prominent businessman, was asked by my father to represent him in the ceremony. Mr. Ong was given a free hand where expenses were concerned. It was superb.

My parents-in-law came from Amoy with the bride and were satisfied with the bridegroom who from an unpolished youth had become a perfect gentleman. After their honeymoon, we all returned to Medan. Third Sister was accompanied by a servant girl, Chui-hua and Lim-mah, her hairdresser.

Ignorant of her new country and its people, Third Sister began her life with a mother-in-law who found fault in everything.

Lim-mah had bound feet and naturally wore her small pointed black embroidered satin shoes with wooden heels while Chui-hua, like all the other servants in Amoy, was shod in black cloth shoes and white socks. So, every movement on the floor above was detectable by the mistress of the house who considered it unfit for servants to work with shoes on. It would have been easier for the servant girl to change her shoes for slippers but for Lim-mah with her bound feet, it was an impossibility.

'How they must stink,' my mother had commented.

Thus the troubles began with the servants. As the servants were criticised, so was Third Sister who was told how lazy she was to have servants at her beck and call. And to have somebody just to do her hair that was unforgivable.

Brother Fa-liong and Third Sister on their wedding day.

Brother Fa-liong and Third Sister in Kobe, Japan.

As my husband and I had to do, the newly weds were to present tea every morning before breakfast. In order to be ready on time, they had to rise very early. My mother complained of the noise made upstairs, disturbing her sleep though she was herself an early riser. In attempting to pacify her, my father dispensed with the custom. But instead, this sent her into an unreasonable fury, saying that her daughter-in-law was never taught manners by her parents. After this everything went wrong.

From then onwards, Third Sister had to be in the kitchen with Kong-soh, our widowed sister-in-law and Po-soh even though she could not cook. She did her best to please her mother-in-law. She helped to wash the vegetables and peel the onions. The latter made her eyes water. Seeing this, my mother observed sarcastically:

'You can be sorry now for your mother's negligence to teach you the necessary, but save your precious tears for some other time.'

Fa-liong was now installed in the small office adjacent to my father's. They observed the same office hours and took their meals together, therefore the young couple seldom saw each other in the day. Since she arrived in Medan, Third Sister had not gone out even once with her husband. One afternoon, Fa-liong, after obtaining permission from our mother, took his wife for a drive to our country house in Poeloe Brayan where he showed her their private zoo. He loved animals.

'My father promised to let me stay here after my marriage,' he told his wife.

'That would be nice,' Third Sister said hopefully.

On the way home, they stopped at the Medan Warenhuis (a department store) to buy cakes for my mother. Returning home, they went upstairs where Third Sister arranged the cakes neatly on a silver plate. Then, both came down again, one carrying the cakes and the other a silver tray and a tea set. Setting them in front of my mother, Fa-liong invited her to taste the cakes, while Third Sister poured the tea. With a rough gesture, my mother pushed the plate of cakes away, saying spitefully: 'Who wants your leftovers! Why didn't you come straight to me? You now give me what's left!'

Third Sister was too stunned to explain. It would not have helped matters even if she did, because once my mother got into a bad mood, there was nothing that could stop her. They stood in silence until she had finished. Third Sister's eyes were brimming with tears. She would not have been able to hold them back much longer.

'Oh! cakes from the Medan Warenhuis!' Djamboel burst in, 'Come Kwet, Ah-chew.'

Without much ado, he grabbed the biggest piece while his younger brother and nephew took the smaller ones. It became the children's tea party. Third Sister served her appreciative young brothers-in-law and nephew who, did not realise that they had averted a storm for which their new sister-in-law was grateful.

In spite of my mother's incessant nagging, Third Sister never complained to us. We thought that everything was in perfect harmony until the day Lim-mah and Chui-hua appeared, with all their luggage, at our front door. They could not bear to stay in the Big House any longer. Everything that they did was wrong in the eyes of the mistress of the house and it was especially so after they would not discard their footwear. They stayed with us until they returned to Amoy with Hoon-ah my Chinese maid a few months later.

7

Baby Adek's hazardous introduction into the world

A FEW MONTHS passed without any further incidents. Third Sister seemed happier now that she was no longer the cause of my mother's annoyance. They were both with child. Third Sister's first and my mother's seventh.

In the beginning of 1919, Third Sister gave birth to a daughter much to her disappointment. My father consoled her by saying that my mother's first child (meaning me) was also a girl and the sons came after.

The grandparents celebrated the first month ceremony as if it was for a grandson; distributing chicken cooked in wine to friends and relatives.

Third Sister's baby Anjoek was a 'cry baby'. She cried for no reason whatsoever, being neither hungry nor sick. All through the night she would cry. Her exasperated mother would cradle the baby in her arms until both fell asleep exhausted — the baby from crying and the mother from cradling.

My mother, losing her patience, said to Third Sister: 'You should do what I did with your sister-in-law when she was a baby. I got so irritated that one night I simply left her under the *djambu* tree. She stopped from then on.'

But Third Sister had not the courage to imitate her mother-in-law. What would happen if Third Sister actually did that to my mother's grand-daughter?

In November that year, Adek (Tsoeng-liong) was born. I shall never forget that day as long as I live.

When my mother went into labour, the midwife was summoned by telephone but before she arrived, the baby was born. Besides the doctor, I was the only one in attendance. The doctor, who thought I was experienced in such matters having a four-year-old son of my own, put the slimy new-born baby into my arms.

'Wash the baby,' he ordered and turned his attention to my mother.

Bewildered, I approached the bath tub filled with warm water and dipped the baby into it. Not knowing how to hold it, it slipped from my hands and submerged in the water. In a frenzy, I pulled the baby out by its neck and held it with trembling hands. I carried the baby to the table, dried it with a towel, put some clothes on it and carried it to my mother's bed. During all this time (it seemed an eternity to me) the baby never made a sound. It lay limply against my breast. I put a finger under its nose. I felt no breath. I was in a panic.

'Put him on his pillow, Foek,' I heard my mother say.

'Yes, Mama,' I answered feebly, but I held the baby even tighter in my arms. What if I had killed it, I thought.

Tears trickled down my cheeks. Dr. van Hengel had left after having congratulated my father. I rocked the bundle in my arms but it gave no sign of life. I felt like fainting, clinging to my charge and praying silently to God to save my little brother. Suddenly it was as if my prayers were answered, the baby gave its first cry!

'Put your little brother down,' my mother said again.

'I would like to hold him in my arms, Ma. Let me, for a little while more,' my words were hardly audible.

8

The ominous die of Fate is cast

DURING THIS PERIOD, my husband enjoyed immense popularity among his Hokkien compatriots because he came from such an illustrious family. They asked him to head the Hua Siong School Board and urged him to set up a new bank.

'I'm going to interview a man whom I am contemplating employing for the new bank,' he told me one day.

'Do you think it's right for you to compete with the Deli Bank where you're the managing director?' I asked.

'There's no question of competition, we'll work together. Your father knows about it and he has given me his approval,' he answered confidently.

'Why are you telling me all this then — you know I'm not interested in business.'

'I just want you to have a look at the person when he comes to see me in the pavilion.'

Hidden behind the bamboo curtains, I could observe, without being seen, the visitor when he passed under the balcony of my drawing room. I don't know why but I did not like his looks which seemed full of cunning and insincerity.

After he had gone, my husband asked with apparent enthusiasm: 'Well, have you seen Mr. Thiam?'

'Yes, but I don't think he's suitable for the job,' I answered.

'Oh, but you don't know him yet. He's extremely clever, a good talker and has had wide experience in the banking business. I need such a man.'

'Can't you find somebody else?' I cried.

'There's no other candidate,· my husband replied, slightly impatient with my poor knowledge of business affairs.

Author's husband King in uniform (1932).

Cousin Pu-ching, Uncle Yong-hian's eldest son.

The next day I had an unexpected visit from Uncle Chooi-lye who was chief cashier at the Nederlandsche Handelmaatschappij (Netherlands Trading Co.).

'I heard that your husband is starting a new bank and is going to employ Mr. Thiam as the manager.'

'That's what he told me,' I looked at my uncle questioningly.

'My advice is that you tell your husband to look for somebody else. We know Mr. Thiam and his past activities aren't quite favourable.'

With this Uncle Chooi-lye left, unwilling to give more detailed information.

When my husband came home, I told him about my uncle's visit.

'But I've already engaged Mr. Thiam.'

'If you were in such a hurry and had already made up your mind, why did you ask my opinion in the first place? Well, you do what you like,' I said irritably. 'I don't like the man.'

Papa had recently handed me the title deeds of the ten shophouses he gave me as part of my dowry. My husband had rented two of the houses at four hundred guilders per month for the premises of the Kong Siong Bank. Thus, including the rent from the remaining eight houses I had a monthly income of nearly one thousand guilders. I felt very happy and rich, completely independent, and spent the money as I wished.

The first month passed and my husband was quite satisfied with the course of affairs at the Kong Siong Bank. All was well and gradually my presentiment evaporated.

With the appointment of cousin Pu-ching as Consul of the Republic of China, it seemed that the younger generation of the family had come into their own glory. Befitting his new social status, the eldest son of Uncle Yong-hian converted the old residence into the Consulate. There, cousin Pu-ching lived with his family, enjoying respect from the community and immunity from the law.

His brothers Kung-we, Kung-lip and Kung-tat often painted the town red with their extravagant living. Their wives competed among themselves, attempting to outdo one

Birthday party of Madam Tsi, mother-in-law of cousin San-jin.

another in clothes and jewellery. When they paraded in the streets of Medan, it was always in the most recent models of imported cars: Hudsons and Cadillacs. They made heads turn with envy, causing unnecessary gossip and criticism. They were parvenu who had neither regard for their elders' hard earned money nor respect for their heritage. Industrious Aunt Hsi (Uncle Yong-hian's village wife) endured it all. She saved and was frugal, never envied the luxury of others and was above all criticism.

Oblivious to the First World War that was then raging in Europe, the younger set continued to indulge in divertissements. It was at this time that a game of chance called *Pei-bin* (eight faces) was introduced by professional gamblers from Penang. It was regarded as innocent entertainment and soon became the craze of the people of Medan. Gradually, this novelty found its way among the elite of society, spinning a web and ensnaring the careless in its powers. The die of Fate had been cast ....

Nothing seemed to go right after that. Business was going from bad to worse. War time gains dwindled and the commercial sector suffered. Through it all, the invisible vermin of Pei-bin continued its work. Some hoped for a miracle.

Pei-bin (eight-face game).

Part Five

1

The broken lamp

THE YEAR WAS 1920. Business deteriorated from day to day. The Kong Siong Bank committed itself to loans it could not meet. Mr. Thiam with his so-called 'wide experiences' in banking showed his true colours. The miracle seemed further than ever. But there were happy times. Papa's sixtieth birthday was a great event. According to ancient belief when a man reached the age of sixty, he is considered to have attained the age of longevity.

On the fourth day of the seventh moon, although it had not been announced outside the family circle, relatives and close friends were gathered in the front hall to wish Papa a long and happy life on his birthday.

A few months later in November, my parents' silver wedding anniversary was celebrated. This time, it was strictly a family affair. Papa had not wanted people to spend money on presents. He reserved that privilege for himself and gave Mama an exquisite emerald necklace set with blue-white diamonds. Though she had received many beautiful things from Papa, this one was unique because it was a token of their twenty-five years of life together.

That evening, sitting around the marble-topped ebony table, Papa, the inseparable cousin Pu-ching, cousin-in-law Tsi Kun-kok, my husband and I were engaged in animated conversation. Papa was drinking champagne and challenging the younger generation to a 'finger game'.

From the back hall, the rest of the family celebrated. Happy laughter could be heard as Djamboel played the clown. Fa-liong was upstairs in the ballroom, with his schoolmates.

Group photograph taken at Father's sixtieth birthday (1920).

They were gathered around the grand piano, executing their self-styled chamber concert.

It was almost like the old days and everyone was relaxed and happy. At the height of the festivity, a cut-glass shade fell from the chandelier hanging above us and shattered on the marble table. All eyes turned to Papa. The broken glass splinters had barely missed him. The noise brought the servants running.

'Just clean it up,' Papa said calmly, still holding his glass of champagne. There was not a sign of misgiving in his tone.

Cousin Pu-ching raised his eyebrows in my husband's direction as if he wanted to tell him something. Someone had the presence of mind to propose a toast. Glasses were brought and together we drank to Papa's good health.

Later that night, as we were each returning to our respective homes, cousin Pu-ching whispered to my husband: 'A bad omen!'

'What do you mean?' my husband asked.

'The broken lamp.'

❦

2

Mama's loyalty

THE TWELFTH MOON was a busy time at the Big House.
This was an annual spring cleaning time when every nook
and cranny was carefully dusted. The old red banners and
scrolls in front of altars of the ancestors and various deities
worshipped in the house were replaced with new ones. The
God of the Kitchen was pompously dispatched up to Heaven
where he was to report to the Celestial Emperor of the good
and bad behaviour of members of the household. He would
be welcomed back on New Year's eve to take his usual place in
the niche of the kitchen.

One Sunday, on his way to the country house in Poeloe
Brayan, Papa took Mama to Hindu Street.

Papa pointed to the buildings, saying to Mama, 'There
are twelve houses here which I'm going to put in your name.
They will be your private property…'

'Why? I don't want property of my own. Isn't it the same if
they remain in your name?' Mama interrupted.

'Certainly there's a difference,' Papa answered.

'But I don't want them.' Mama snapped, beginning to get
annoyed.

Papa sighed at her ignorance. But was it ignorance or loyalty?

'If I happen to die…' He tried to explain.

'I don't want you to talk like that!' Mama turned away
angrily ordering the driver to go on.

In Poeloe Brayan, the Japanese overseer Makakeba was
waiting to take his employer for a stroll round the picturesque
estate. They went past the zoo then reached the riverside.

'We must strengthen the dike, boss, to prevent a flood like we had the last time when we had to use sampans to reach the main road.'

'Certainly, you know best,' said Papa.

'If I could have your permission…' the Japanese continued.

'I leave the work in your hands.'

Before going back to the house where lunch was being prepared, they stopped at the Sacred Lake. White water lilies grew in abundance between the reeds covering the surface of the water.

'Poor boy!' Papa sighed remembering Colonel Bleckman's son who was drowned there many years ago. 'It seems as if his spirit lives in those flowers!' Papa wiped away an involuntary tear. A vision of his own dead son Kong-liong, whose mother lay buried by the riverside, emerged before his eyes. Memories of his own boyhood surged from within him. How keen he was then to go into the far and wide world, to make money, to attain power and fame, to build a house of his own in the old village to spend the rest of his days. Now he had accomplished more than he bargained for and yet…

3

The nocturnal visitor

WE BEGAN TO receive visits from a mysterious nocturnal visitor. A huge toad, with an enormous white belly and rough brownish back marked with grey specks like buttons, would stare at us with glistening eyes from under the hat stand in the front gallery. In the morning it would be gone. When it first appeared, we found it amusing but when it came every night, I became scared.

'Strange,' my husband said one evening, 'where does this tailless animal come from? I've never seen it come or go.'

'Maybe it's a bad spirit, disguised,' I whispered.

'Nonsense!' he laughed. 'On the contrary, it might be a good fairy bringing us luck.'

'Then don't chase it away.' So we left it alone.

One evening, Papa told us that he had received the blueprint of a ship he had ordered from Japan. It was to be 6,000 tons and both a pleasure and cargo vessel. He told us that we were all to go to Europe on its maiden voyage. I was thrilled. To see Europe and to know strange places and people was always my dream.

'We go sailing,' he said in English.

'Wonderful, Papa, your English has improved,' I praised.

'Your father is an intelligent pupil,' he laughed in merriment and we joined in heartily.

As he wished us 'good-night', he promised to show us the blueprint the following evening.

We retired at about 10 o'clock.

As if in a dream, I heard a voice calling my name.

'*Non, Non Besar* (Miss, Big miss),' I heard in my sleep. Then I was awake and recognised my father's syce's voice.

'*Ya* (yes),' I answered.

As I pushed aside the bamboo curtain and peered out into the darkness, Amat's silhouette was barely discernible and I asked apprehensively: 'What is it?'

'*Nonya Besar panggil, Tuan Besar tidak enak badan.* (The Mistress is calling, Master is not feeling well.)'

All of a sudden, I was trembling, feeling the cold night air.

'What's going on?' my husband's voice reached me from the bed.

'Papa is unwell,' I replied, still shivering.

'He was alright when he left us tonight,' my husband said.

I did not hear him. I had already gone downstairs to the waiting car.

***

I went straight to Papa's room. Mama sat on the bed, holding Papa's hand.

'Have you any pain? I heard you calling out loudly,' Mama asked. Papa gave a deep sigh.

'No, no pain, I'm just worried,' he said, breathing heavily.

'Worried about what?'

'If only Kung-tat could pay the Deli Bank, he had overdrawn…'

'Don't think about business now. Here's the doctor.'

Dr. van Hengel examined Papa while Mama and I watched anxiously.

'You're alright, Major, you're only tired and need a good rest. Working too hard. I'll drop in first thing in the morning. See that he doesn't get up until I come,' he cautioned my mother. With these words, the doctor left the room. I followed him out.

'What's it, doctor?' I asked.

'I can't say for sure at the moment, all he needs now is rest.' Both my half-sisters had joined me outside my father's room. We heard Papa say to Mama, 'The baby needs you. You had better go to him.'

'Go to sleep now, you heard what the doctor said,' Mama said gently.

She climbed out of the bed and let down the mosquito net.

'You three had better stay around. If anything happens, call me,' she whispered as she passed us.

We sat on the cement floor reading each other's faces in silence. We heard Papa's regular breathing, followed soon after by his snoring; a sure sign that he had fallen into a deep slumber. We assured each other that Papa would be alright.

4

The graveyard

AT SIX O'CLOCK Mama came to us and said: 'Your father is sleeping well. Foek, get ready to go to Pengkalan Brandan. I don't think I'll go but take your cousin Fu-jin with you. Song-jin and Kwei-jin, go to sleep now. I'll ask Kario (my father's native valet) to keep watch.'

I went home to prepare for the trip to Brandan.

'How's your father?' asked my husband.

'The doctor said Papa must have complete rest for a few days, he's overworked. I'm going to the graves of my grandparents with my cousin. Today is the twenty-seventh of the twelfth moon, the last day for offerings before the New Year.'

'Alright, I'll go over to see your father before I go to the office.' I picked up cousin Fu-jin at Aunt Hsi's house in the yellow Fiat Mama had put at our disposal.

The sun was already up, but somehow we felt cold though wrapped in woollen shawls. I told my cousin about Papa's indisposition.

'Perhaps he had a nightmare,' she said.

'Possible, but my mother said that the cry he gave was so unusually loud that it scared her.'

'Let's pray it's nothing.'

We turned our thoughts to the coming New Year in three days' time. I told her that I had bought a new evening dress of black taffeta embroidered with gold roses and trimmed with gold lace for the New Year's reception for foreigners.

'I paid 250 guilders for it at Toko Duson.'

'You're extravagant in your dresses but I'm going to gamble on New Year's Day because if I win on the first day of the year,

I'll have good luck the whole year through,' she said naively.

The ride took one and a half hours. When we reached the Hai Lok-Hong private graveyard, its keeper was already there waiting with the offerings my mother had ordered a few days before. We climbed slowly up the slope to my grandparents Lim's graves.

Author and cousin Fu-jin.

After we finished praying, a great quantity of silver paper was burned. Great flames shot up and ashes danced around the open space, a happy sign that the offerings were being accepted by the spirits. We left the graveyard after giving orders that the meat, fowl, fish and cakes be distributed among the keeper and his coolies. It was not yet 9 o'clock.

A coolie on a bicycle stopped us at the crossroad near the resthouse. Stepping down he said to me: '*Non* is asked to go back to Medan immediately and not stop at the resthouse. I just received this instruction a while ago.'

Although I had not intended to go to the resthouse that morning, the urgency of the message surprised me, making me feel uneasy.

'Papa must have gotten worse.' I thought to myself. We continued the journey in silence, broken occasionally by my order to the driver to go faster.

When we reached the Big House I noticed much activity in the house. Then I saw Djamboel running towards us. Before the car could stop, he said: 'Papa is dead.'

5

The fallen tree

I STARED AT Djamboel, speechless.

Someone pulled me out of the car and led me into the house. I moved as in a trance. I was made to kneel at the foot of a couch. At the right side of the ancestral hall, a body lay clothed in a long blue gown topped by a short black satin jacket. The body looked like Papa, his face was unchanged, his eyes tightly closed but his lips were slightly parted as if to speak, once again; but I heard nothing.

'Here,' said someone near me, 'put these socks on your father.' Mechanically I put the white socks on my father's right, then left foot. Then I was given a close fitting black satin hat to put on his head. Yes, it was my father before me, so it was true — Papa *is* dead. I buried my face in the folds of his wide sleeves, sobbing.

'Pull her away,' someone cried, 'don't let her tears fall on his body, it will make his going away harder, she's his favourite child.' Then I heard nothing more.

I was sitting on the stone floor, slumped against the door of my mother's room, when I regained consciousness. Someone was rubbing me with medicated oil, while someone handed me a drink. Slowly, my eyes focused and I saw my husband bending over me.

'Are you alright?' he asked softly.

I nodded. Then I saw little brother Tseong-liong near an earthen vessel burning silver paper with his bigger brothers and sisters. His face was smudged with soot. While other mourners sniffed and sobbed, he regarded them with his soft big eyes wondering why they were crying. Nobody took the trouble to clean the little face which so earnestly and devotedly looked at each piece of silver paper as it was put in the fire. They were being burnt to supply his father with money on his journey to Eternity.

A huge shadow fell across me and a trembling hand touched my shoulder.

'Foekje!'

It was Oom Onnes.

I fell at his feet crying uncontrollably.

'My father-in-law died of apoplexy, Mr. Onnes,' my husband informed him. 'When my mother-in-law went in to see him, he was already beyond help. The doctor arrived only in time to certify his death.'

'I could not come earlier, I was at Si Boelan,' Oom Onnes stammered, hardly able to hide his emotion.

The great man whom he was destined to meet when he was downtrodden by society had come to him as a friend. This friend had trusted him with more than thirty of his flourishing estates, where before, he was not even considered for the post of third assistant in the smallest plantation.

This great man was Tjong A Fie, his friend, now gone! His bulky frame convulsed with sobs, he turned towards the immobile figure on the couch.

6

The scattering leaves

MY FATHER DIED on the twenty-seventh day of the twelfth moon, Year of the Monkey, February 8th 1921.

The following morning at nine his body was laid in a heavy mahogany coffin in the ancestral hall. An auspicious hour was to be chosen to close the cover which would forever deprive us of contemplating the beloved face. Kneeling on the stone floor, we surrounded the coffin, lamenting in grief that the one we loved was gone forever.

At 10 o'clock, Notary Fouquain de Grave and his deputy Tjeerd Dykstra, accompanied by their native clerk, arrived for the reading of my father's will.

We were all assembled in my father's dining hall where the two Dutchmen were seated at the round marble table with my mother and Fa-liong on either side of them.

The Notary broke the seal and began to read in Dutch while the clerk translated it into Malay so that everyone could understand the will's contents.

All my father's descendants, male and female, were provided for without exception. So were his adopted son and grandson, Po-liong and Toeng-ngee. (They were not adopted under Dutch law and thus the adoption was actually void but none of us realised it then.)

My father had appointed his wife Lim Koei-yap sole 'executrix testamentaire' and guardian of his minor children.

After deducting the properties given to his daughters as dowry, all his wordly goods, movable and unmovable, were to go into a foundation named *Stichting Toen Moek Tong* which was to be established at his death in Medan, the Netherlands

Indies and in Sung-kow, his village in the province of Kwantung.

His male descendants mentioned in the will were legal heirs to the foundation which could not be divided, dissolved or sold. They were to receive a percentage of the usufruct for their livelihood, a percentage for the maintenance of the ancestors' home and a percentage to be given to charities. Each would get 150,000 guilders on their marriage. If one of the heirs was incapacitated by illness, deformed at birth or mentally deranged, the foundation was to support him during his lifetime... The will could not be contested no matter what the circumstances.

After the reading, the Notary made us all sign a document honoring the will.

Author's mother.

At 12 o'clock, the officer from the department for orphans called to probe my father's vast inheritance but after seeing my father's last testament, there was nothing left for him to do but to withdraw.

In the afternoon, Oom Onnes came to see my mother.

'Have courage, Madam,' he said, 'you must have strength for the big task that lies before you, don't let grief run its free course.'

'How can I manage it all alone?' Mama asked doubtfully.

'Whenever you need me, I'll be by your side. How else can I ever repay your husband's generosity but by my loyalty?'

For the next two weeks, my mother went about like a whirlwind, running from one government office to another, attending court and visiting banks. She, who had always enjoyed a sheltered life, found the responsibilities of an 'executrix testamentaire' night-marish. Fortunately, there was Oom Onnes to inspire her with strength and confidence.

'Be assured, Madam, the Major shall have a funeral befitting his standing. I've extracted a promise from the Javasche Bank to let you have a free hand in the matter. Were we to sacrifice all else, no expense shall be spared for the funeral.'

'You've done well, my friend, we owe it to him.'

7

The farewell

PUN-CHUNG, Abbot of the *Kek Lok Si* in Ayer Itam, had arrived from Penang with twelve monks to say the funeral prayers for my father who had contributed so generously when the temple was being built.

Tien Hau Kung, temple of the Goddess of the Sea in Medan, built by uncles Yong-hian and You-hian, was chosen as the site for funeral prayers and ceremonies. They were to last forty-nine days.

In the centre of a vast enclosure, a platform was erected to hold a beautifully embroidered picture of the Three Buddhas: the Present, Past and Future. Below it was one of the Buddha, Saviour of the Souls. The traditional 'Home of the Spirit' was a magnificent structure of bamboo laths and multicoloured paper with decorations of silks and tinsel. It had the aspect of a real manor complete with paper effigies of men, horses, carriages, sedan chairs and automobiles. Its gate was guarded by the Four Guardians of the Gate of Heaven: four gigantic statues of fearsome countenance.

All these paper articles were made by expert craftsmen and would go into flames on the forty-ninth day, on the termination of the prayers and ceremonies; it being the deceased's spirit's last day on earth before departing for the Realm of Hades — region of the Ten Kings who decide the fate of mortals in the after life.

At the front of the 'Home of the Spirit' was a long table displayed with incense, flowers and offerings. A wooden drum and tinkling bell provided solemn music as the twelve monks chanted the sutras, morning, noon and evening.

People of all walks of life packed the temple day and night to observe the unique ceremonies. They were especially awestruck at the sight of two tableax. The first depicted Heaven filled with colourful clouds and a rainbow inhabited by the Eight Immortals who lead good people to the celestial sphere. The other showed the netherworld with demons dragging evil ones to Hell. These were punished in cauldrons of boiling oil, chased up the Mountain of Knives or thrown into the Pool of Blood and Snakes. Here, their souls would linger indefinitely until the day of Reincarnation and the Great Judgment in Heaven and Earth.

Beggars lined the roadsides waiting to pick up offerings of food put out at the end of each ceremony.

Everyone mourned the deceased who in his lifetime had been a friend to all including the poor and crippled...

***

My father's coffin had been painted and repainted seven times with tung oil from China to preserve it. It would be resistant to damp and vermin for a hundred years. The tomb itself was chosen by a master of geomancy. It was built of cement and lined with lead walls making it impenetrable to water.

Days before the funeral people came from near and far, from Atjeh in the north and Padang in the west, from the whole east coast of Sumatra, from Penang, Malaysia, Singapore and Java.

They all came spontaneously to pay their last respects to the man who, in his lifetime, had done unaccountable good deeds to his fellow-men, irrespective of race and nationality.

Before the coffin was placed a photograph of my father dressed in his simple white cotton jacket just as he had been when he arrived from the old country.

Humble, modest people knelt before it in reverence, sobbing uncontrollably like forlorn and lost children. The Tree that had given them shade and shelter had fallen...

The cortege was endless. Everyone accompanied this great man on his last journey to his eternal resting place.

House of Spirit.

Pavilion of Longevity and Happiness.

The closed tomb robbed the mourners of their immortal friend but left them with an unforgettable memory.

***

Yes, the tree had fallen, branches broken, leaves scattered in the four corners of the world, but the roots remain unscathed; deeply embedded in the soil awaiting benevolent sunshine and rain to make them sprout anew in a strong generation of the sons of Cathay.

He is gone for decades now. He may be already forgotten in the dimmed glory of the past; however, in some remote spot in this world, his name may yet ring a familiar echo.

Like his contemporaries, his spirit is perpetuated in the memorable life-like statue enshrined in the Tower of Sacred Books in the *Kek Lok Si* of Ayer Itam.

Old-timers, hard-working pioneers who had adopted the Southern Seas as their motherland had left their heritage in the establishments of clans. Likewise, this stolid figure from Sung-kow, having tasted all the sweetness and aridness of life had built the Big House in Medan to unite his descendants under that tree.

Epilogue

IT WAS PAPA'S wish that we live in the Big House as a family and we fulfilled it for him. Today, Kwet-liong's, Lee-liong's, Tsoeng-liong's families and myself live in those rooms steeped with warm images of the past.

There are yet many more memories which I cherish that span the year of my father's death up till today. To commit them all in detail to paper is my sincere wish, but I am eighty-four this year — time has been a gracious host to me, but she is no longer on my side. How does one capture the nuances of sixty years in a brief chapter? The words will be a mere shadow of the real things found within me...

My husband was never destined to be the businessman he hoped to be. After the many failures he suffered in Medan he needed distractions and a change of environment. We therefore travelled extensively for five years, taking in the sights and sounds of China. It was during this time in Hangchow, on the West Lake, that my love for the Chinese culture and literature deepened. It was there I learned about the history of the Sung dynasty with its unforgettable happenings.

Inspired by the beauty of the surroundings, my husband completed at that time his book of poems which is being widely read in Amoy and Taiwan today.

It was 1926 when we finally returned to Father-in-law's home in Kulangsu (Amoy). My parents-in-law were both in poor health and a German doctor advised Father-in-law to go to a Swiss sanatorium for treatment and rest.

That year saw the realisation of one of my fondest dreams — we were going for an extended stay in Europe. We spent six grand years on the continent using Arosa, the snow-covered hill resort in the Swiss Alps, as our base. There I learnt the German language, adding it to my knowledge of Dutch and French.

Each summer we toured Southern Europe. I remember Venice in Italy. How the canals, gondolas, grand palaces and charming people captured my romantic senses.

Father-in-law and his entourage created a sensation everywhere we went. There were few Chinese seen in Europe in those days. Being the only one in the group to speak European languages, I was especially useful to everyone.

It was a great pity that Mother-in-law who would have joined us the year following our arrival in Arosa died without having her hope realised.

My knowledge of languages secured me my first job when we returned to China in 1931. I was, for three years, a liaison-officer with the Ministry of Foreign Affairs in Nankin which was headed by Dr. C. T. Wang. In this department, I had ample opportunity to become acquainted with other Chinese officials as well as ambassadors and dignitaries of many countries. Of all the people I met officially, the most surprised was Prof. Duivendak, a Sinologist. He was Dutch and was delighted to meet a Chinese lady government officer who could converse with him in his native tongue.

The next official position I held was given me by my mother. She sent me to Swatow to investigate the business connected with the railway my father and Uncle Yong-hian had established. How important I felt to be managing director of such an essential facility in public transport. How strange the people thought it was to have a woman in such an important position.

It was such a painful thing to do — to break up the railway, but it had to be done and I drew strength from knowing that Papa would have done likewise in a similar situation. The Sino-Japanese war had erupted and the Guomingtang government had ordered that the railway be demolished to stop the Japanese advance. When the Japanese troops eventually landed in Swatow, my husband who was then in Taiwan left together with his friends for Manchukuo (Manchuria). I was evacuated to Hong Kong and eventually returned to Medan. I was never to see my husband again. He died in Manchukuo in 1940 of lung cancer. I could not get to him or attend his funeral. His ashes were brought back to Father-in-law in Shanghai.

World War Two broke out. Surging like a flood which could not be stemmed, the Japanese invaded Indonesia which they occupied for three and a half years. The long awaited liberation came only in 1945.

I was again sent to Swatow to inquire after the railway. It was never rebuilt. Instead, a highway was laid out and our family managed a fleet of buses which ran on it. Things seemed to be turning for the Tjongs, when again a twist of Fate intervened in yet another form. The Communist government came to power in China. Once more I escaped to Medan while my husband's family followed the Guomingtangs to Taiwan. For the next two decades I travelled throughout Indonesia and went at intervals to visit my in laws in Taiwan.

My son Tong who had become a Singaporean applied unsuccessfully for me to be granted permanent resident status in Singapore in 1958. Two years later he contracted mouth cancer. In spite of the best treatment, he succumbed at last to this fearsome disease. He was reduced to skin and bone but bore all with stoicism. His death broke the vital link in the chain between myself and future generations.

Mama lived to a ripe old age. She was ninety-three when she died in 1972. Sister Sze-yin, Lee-liong's widow and I cared for her till the very end. She told us she wanted a grand funeral and was given one. How moved we were when we realised that her passing was as deeply felt by the Medan community as when Papa died fifty-one years ago. Thousands came to pay their last respects, including the Sultan and his family.

In 1974, I visited Europe again and with each familiar place, memories began to filter through. Happy and nostalgic scenes came alive with the voices and laughter of those gone before me. It was with this frame of mind that I came home to Medan.

This mood went with me to Brastagi, a hill resort belonging to Lee Rubber where I now spend most of my time. I feel much comforted and fulfilled when I remember that it was in this serenity that I was inspired to write my memoirs.

Family Tree

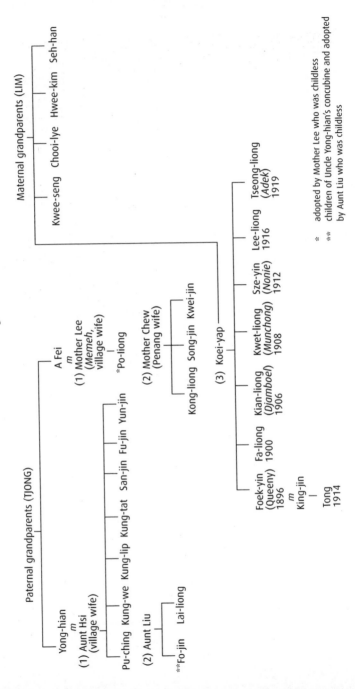

Paternal grandparents (TJONG)

Maternal grandparents (LIM)

Kwee-seng Chooi-lye Hwee-kim Seh-han

Yong-hian
m
(1) Aunt Hsi
(village wife)

Pu-ching Kung-we Kung-lip Kung-tat

(2) Aunt Liu

**Fo-jin Lai-liong

A Fei
m
(1) Mother Lee
(*Memeh*,
village wife)

*Po-liong

(2) Mother Chew
(Penang wife)

Kong-liong Song-jin Kwei-jin

San-jin Fu-jin Yun-jin

(3) Koei-yap

Foek-yin
(*Queeny*)
1896
m
King-jin

Tong
1914

Fa-liong
1900

Kian-liong
(*Djamboel*)
1906

Kwet-liong
(*Munchong*)
1908

Sze-yin
(*Nonie*)
1912

Lee-liong
1916

Tseong-liong
(*Adek*)
1919

* adopted by Mother Lee who was childless
** children of Uncle Yong-hian's concubine and adopted
by Aunt Liu who was childless

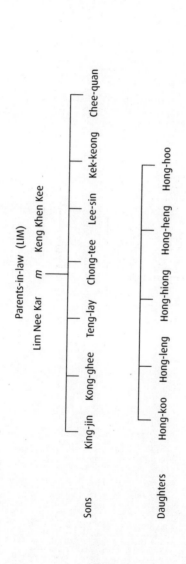

Parents-in-law (LIM)

Lim Nee Kar   *m*   Keng Khen Kee

Sons

King-jin Kong-ghee Teng-lay Chong-tee Lee-sin Kek-keong Chee-quan

Daughters

Hong-koo Hong-leng Hong-hiong Hong-heng Hong-hoo